Mercy's Heroes

"Mercy is about getting to know, to meet, real heroes. Street-slum smart, sometimes almost broken kids, but Mercy loves and serves them. Children, beaten down, whom nothing, no one, can break, except to be laughed at or scorned. Tom's stories bring out the reality, the pain, the courage of these children as they kick open the door. Their own stories that cry out to be told. Stories that, without Tom's listening and care through fourteen years of love and service to the hearts of our Mercy children, would have remained silent. And thank goodness Tom listened, captured their dreams and hopes, and tells their story in this book."

—Fr. Joseph H. Maier, CSsR

"Visiting the Mercy Centre in Bangkok always restored my faith in the resilience of people in the face of adversity and the importance of supporting that resilience in any way I could. I saw as much energy and talent amongst those using the facilities of the Mercy Centre as in any place in the world. They just needed a chance to shine and a hand up, not a handout. I was delighted to support in any way I could, and whatever supporters could do was more than returned in the progress made and the lives enhanced. I am delighted that Tom has taken the time to document the work of the centre."

—Ambassador Brendan Rogers, formerly ambassador of Ireland to Thailand

"*Mercy's Heroes* is a gut-punch to the soul. Tom Crowley's no-nonsense, compelling narrative vividly reveals the horrendous conditions and the all-too-likely dead-end future of kids living in the poorest slums of Bangkok. Yet, in the middle of this bleak environment stands Mercy Centre, a charity dedicated to helping these kids get food, an education, and hope for a better future. There is so much more to Crowley's story, but at its heart are the accounts of the smiling resilience of the children, and of the selfless work of Mercy's staff against never-ending impossible odds and challenges that is nothing short of inspirational."

—Dwight Jon Zimmerman, #1 *New York Times* bestselling author

Mercy's Heroes:
The Fight for Human Dignity in the Bangkok Slums

by Tom Crowley

ISBN 978-1-64663-535-1

Published by

 köehlerbooks™

3705 Shore Drive
Virginia Beach, VA 23455
800-435-4811
www.koehlerbooks.com

Mercy's Heroes

THE **FIGHT** FOR **HUMAN DIGINITY** IN THE **BANCKOK SLUMS**

TOM CROWLEY

VIRGINIA BEACH
CAPE CHARLES

ALSO BY
TOM CROWLEY

Fiction

The Matt Chance Thrillers
Viper's Tail
Murder in the Slaughterhouse
Bangkok Gamble

Non-Fiction

Bangkok Pool Blues
Shrapnel Wounds

Dedicated to Sr. Mary Sean, School Sisters of Notre Dame,
a teacher who changed lives.

"Let the little children come to me, and do not hinder them, for the kingdom of heaven belongs to such as these."

—Matthew 19:14

". . . . how is it that we are not more sensitive to the presence of something greater than ourselves moving forward within us and in our midst?"

—Teilhard de Chardin, The Phenomenon of Man

TABLE OF CONTENTS

FOREWORD

I asked Father Joe to contribute anything he might like to say in print as a foreword. He chose to write about Mercy's first program— a kindergarten in the slums. Today, Mercy has twenty-three kindergartens spread throughout the slums of Bangkok, teaching poor children their first lessons in reading and writing and preparing them for grade school— and life. Here, in his own words, is Fr. Joe.

—Tom Crowley

Dear everyone,

I can't possibly dream of anything more angelic than the pure innocent sounds of 270 kindergarten four- and five- and six-year-olds, mostly Buddhist (a handful of Catholics) kids chanting their daily school morning prayers ending with our beautiful Hail Mary to Our Blessed Virgin Mary, Mother of Jesus, whom they know loves them all.

Opening doors for the ordinary creates the extraordinary.

To kick open the door only once—so it stays open. That's what our Mercy Centre and Human Development Foundation does.

We kick open the door for ordinary slum kids who do not have the slightest chance at scholarships or being placed in "good schools." Scholarships don't typically go to the ordinary poor. And that's what almost all of our kids are: poor and slum-born to parents who are often absent or not worth mentioning. Their only saving grace are their grannies, wizened old souls who have often been beaten, bruised, mocked, you name it.

Because of the grannies, a few mums become stalwart, sturdy, and strong too. One day they will be the matured grannies of the slum. A few dads also mature well. Very few, but one in particular. I won't tell you his name, but he's doing the "family prison time." Pretty Mum was framed by some competition on the street. The competition hid a packet of drugs on her and then ran to tell corrupt cops. Prison for Mum, for sure. Mature Dad stepped up and said, "I'll say the drugs were mine. I will go to prison for you so you and Grannie can raise our child in dignity."

Mature Dad kicked the door open to a better future for his child. Cost him two years in prison, but as he said, "For my son, it's worth it." We at Mercy kept that door open. Mature Dad's son just graduated from our Kindergarten Three. Not the smartest lad in class. A fine-looking kid, but not the most handsome or the most popular or the most athletic. Good and ordinary. It was enough to get him through. Now he's headed into first grade in a proper school. He's an ordinary Klong Toey six-year-old loved by all and who is enriched by all the survival skills gleaned from slum life.

It's been very quiet at the Mercy Centre lately. Just not much news to share. For us, that is usually good news. All is well here as the school year winds down. Nearly 400 kids will soon be graduating from our third-year kindergarten and moving into first grade—a massively big deal when you are of that age. So for kids like our ordinary boy, these days are very exciting, filled with good wishes, prayers, and glorious expectations.

These slum children are moving ahead in their lives today fully able to do basic math and to make change at the 7-Eleven, and they are wily in the technical ways of smart phones, laptops, desktops, social media, and such. They can write their names, say their prayers, and for the most part, read and write. Basic literacy is a huge advantage for first graders.

But beyond these foundational skills, they also possess practical life skills. They all know how to use the commercial washing machines scattered in the many laundromats throughout Klong Toey. How to insert 20 Baht and add soap powder bought for five Baht at the 7-Eleven. And no dryer is needed because they know how to hang wet clothes in the sun to dry.

In so many ways, our ordinary is extraordinary. These kids entering first grade are sturdy, tough, and street wise. It's rare to see them panic and even more rare to see a boy cry. There's a slogan in the slums: "Klong Toey boys don't cry." And it's pretty much true. They fight back or, if they can't win, they run—fast as the wind (smile).

Our children are different from most slum and abandoned children and will likely remain that way for the rest of their lives. Why? Because they are way ahead on the road. From Kindergarten One to Kindergarten Three and heading into first grade, they have thrived in school, they have gone regularly to the doctor, and they were always fed at least one large meal a day in kindergarten. Like basic math, these additions are easily calculated: Well-fed and well-educated ordinary slum children become extraordinarily confident and unafraid. They are proud to be Mercy School grads. Boast about it, even.

Yes, the past year has been very different. Our kids know all too well about the Covid Ugly. They fear the nasty creature, as they should. It continues to rant and rave in the slums of Klong Toey and the other slums of Bangkok, where we have our twenty-two slum kitchens and kindergartens. But streetwise kids wash and wear their masks and keep at a safe distance whenever they can. They are cautious, careful.

So for us at Mercy, it is a day-to-day working miracle seen in real time. There is no other way to explain it. Children, old folks, teachers, cooks, parents, and relatives of some 2,000 children coming to our schools and kitchens every day. We diligently wear our masks, wash our hands, and try to never get too close. That much is understood. But day-to-day miracles require daily nurturing, and we work hard at it. As a wise entrepreneur once said, "Never fall asleep on your success."

So our Mercy comes in daily doses and simple rules: Go to school. Go to school. Go to school. That's Rule Number One. In school, you are safe, you are fed, you are educated, and, most importantly, you are loved. School gives your Granny and Pretty Mum and Mature Dad in prison hope for you to have a better future.

Today, some fifty years after we opened that first slum school in a slaughterhouse pigpen, more than 50,000 kids can read, write, pray, and correctly count their change at the 7-Eleven. They are not unwitting subjects to liars, scam artists and short-changers. School smarts + street smarts = Extraordinary.

We "outsiders," even if we have been here for five decades, need to always be humble. Being "a smarty pants" results in instant failure. Who are we or you or anyone to tell a slaughterhouse kid what life is like when they live every day in a squalid hovel, and we don't? So we have always minded our manners and asked permission to come into the slums. Always asked permission to pay respect to the slum's Sacred Shrine and even to offer flowers and to ask Our Blessed Mother Mary, Mother of Jesus to Bless and protect us all. All of us of all faiths and religions.

After receiving permission from the guardians of the slum—the grannies selling noodles as you enter—we can travel with heroes and cronies alike. That way, we can talk to the kids also. Talk always in front of everyone, never alone, especially to the kids. And we never give anything to anyone—not a donation, alms, not anything—before asking if the person receiving the gift would be offended to receive the gift from us.

With proper respect and humility, we were able to ask anyone and everyone if they would object if their children or grandchildren went to school, right there in the slum, right in the squalor if necessary. No need for legal documents. In case of rain, any shack would do. Or just any open space. Use a large secondhand umbrella against the sun and mats on the ground.

That's how it began. Now, a half-century later, the slum is still a salvage place of sorts, but it is drenched in the Mercy of 50,000 extraordinarily ordinary kids who are among Klong Toey's and even Thailand's very best.

Come, walk with Mercy's Heroes, the Mercy kids, the slum families, and the Mercy staff who walk with the poor on a daily basis to give kids the one chance they need.

To walk on the margins of life is blessed. To be accepted by the Poor is blessed. Let us forge ahead on this blessed walk in the shadow of the rainbow.

INTRODUCTION

Mercy has saved the lives of countless children. There are, around the world, many religious or social welfare organizations named or nicknamed Mercy. The Mercy I write of originated in the slum area of Bangkok, adjacent to the city's port in the early 1970s and continues to the present day. Its formal foundation name is the Human Development Foundation. There have been many heroes, acts of compassion, and heroic community service at Mercy over the years. To me, that makes telling the story, the more then fourteen years of it I witnessed, a requirement.

The book is not meant to be about me as I had only a minor role. But as I am the testifying witness, there is some need to make my role and point-of-view known.

After service as a combat infantry officer in Vietnam, followed by several years in Asian affairs in the Foreign Service and then in business in Asia for over twenty years, I decided in early 1998 to turn my back on the business world and take my life in a different direction. It wasn't an abrupt decision but rather something I had been mulling over for years. Service in Vietnam provided very few "feel good" stories, but for me, those times when we went on MEDCAPS, programs providing medical treatment to the people in small country villages, were of great emotional relief. For once we were doing something good for the Vietnamese people. The kids would gather around, some to get medical treatment. Some, laughing and chatting, came to play in front of the group of foreigners. Those missions were bright spots in the cruel chaos that was combat in Vietnam. While in college after my military service, I had looked into volunteering for a street kids' group in Milwaukee, but found the time away from my studies too much to take on. During my travels in Asia over the two years prior to volunteering with Mercy, I had made several visits and donated to the Christina Noble Foundation, an orphanage and home for street kids in Saigon. Thus, when I decided to make a change in life, it was a proposition I had given some thought to.

At the time, I was living and working in Bangkok. I had heard of the Mercy Centre, a renowned, street-based foundation serving poor families and children in the Bangkok slums. I decided to start there. I called Mercy's office, explained I was an American businessman who desired to step back from the business world, and asked if I could volunteer. The person I spoke with, Tim Haig, a Canadian who had overseen the accounting for Mercy for several years, arranged an appointment for me to meet with Fr. Joe Maier, Mercy's Director, the following morning. Thus, it began.

The public face of Mercy features the main characters who founded it and have guided it since the beginning, Fr. Joe Maier and Sr. Maria Chantavarodom.

Sr. Maria was born in Macau in 1931 and raised in Thailand. Her family came from Guangdong Province, China, to the Portuguese-governed colony of Macau. She received a Catholic education and then joined religious life as a Catholic nun. Sr. Maria is a founding member of The Daughters of the Queenship of Mary Immaculate, and she has served as the Mother Superior of the order for over fifty years. Sr. Maria started her street-based community work, serving the poor, in the area called Jet Sip Rai, the Klong Toey district slum adjacent to the Bangkok port, in 1967.

Fr. Joe was born in South Dakota but grew up in Long View, Washington. He enrolled in a Redemptorist seminary in high school and was educated in religious studies in California and Wisconsin. After being ordained a Redemptorist priest in 1965, he came to Bangkok and then to Pattaya for language study prior to undertaking duties as a missionary priest. After serving several years in Laos, he was ordered back to Bangkok in 1971 to avoid capture as the communists overthrew the Laotian royal government.

At that time, there was an opening for a parish priest in the Immaculate Conception of Mary of Miraculous Medal church in what was called the slaughterhouse area of the Klong Toey slum in Bangkok.

The slaughterhouse area was home to the nightly killing and cleaning of pigs for early morning delivery to fresh markets throughout Bangkok. The slaughterhouse workers were all impoverished Catholics, who comprised Fr. Joe's parishioners.

We see the world as we want or expect it to be. For many who come to know of Mercy, it's common to say, "Oh yes, Fr. Joe." That statement is, of itself, true and at the same time completely wrong. Fr. Joe has dedicated his life to Mercy, and he deserves much of the credit for how magnificent Mercy has become. Much, but not all. I've been a bit amazed over the years to see Western visitors praise Fr. Joe's role and go home completely unaware of Sr. Maria's key role in the establishment, growth and greatness of Mercy. Fr. Joe is a white male and Sr. Maria an Asian woman. Western visitors seem to expect to see a white man as the potential saint, and they completely miss Sr. Maria and go home ignorant of who she is or what she does. Most visitors, whether donors, short-term volunteers, or slum tourists, go home without understanding the value of Sr. Maria's contributions. As she doesn't speak English and doesn't really care to be known outside of Mercy and her religious community, she inadvertently contributes to that lack of recognition.

Fr. Joe is enormously respected, almost worshipped at times, within Mercy. But the staff are virtually all women, and the person they relate to, and fear to disappoint, is Sr. Maria. Their widely different personalities and responsibilities have combined to make Mercy the wonderful refuge and house of love that it is.

As two key Christian religious figures working in the same areas of the slum, Fr. Joe and Sr. Maria were destined to meet. When he arrived in 1971, she came to the church to introduce herself to the new pastor. They spoke frequently of their work in the slum in the following months. In 1972, Sr. Maria, in daily contact with a number of "slum moms," came up with an idea. *Why don't we start a school for the slum kids?* It would be a preschool for kids aged three to six, to give them a basic reading and writing education. Possibly that might be all the school the slum kids ended up getting, but Fr. Joe and Sr. Maria also had the goal of providing these poorest of kids a head start on entering the first grade in public school. Note that this was forty years before education authorities in Thailand had any thought of a preschool program.

Sr. Maria did the recruiting, going from household to household, explaining the school program to the moms, who were the family decision-makers on such things. Enough children, twenty or so, were enrolled to start the first school. The program was well received in the slum area and soon there were requests for a second school, then a third. The teachers came from the pool of moms in the slum area who had basic education (possibly just through sixth grade in those days), women who would understand the children in their care, women who were devoted to making the schools a success. A key part of the program from the beginning was that lunch meals would be prepared and served in the school each day. For some children it might be the only meal they would get that day.

The joining of their efforts by a cohort of slum moms and these two highly respected religious figures was the beginning of what became an enormously beneficial organization for street kids, spreading throughout twenty, at times over thirty, slum areas of Bangkok.

While Fr. Joe and Sr. Maria deserve enormous credit, it is the heroic staff, the children of Mercy and their counselors, that I want to bring to center stage in this book.

The Mercy program soon grew beyond the schools. The slum moms who had become the teachers, working with the kids on a daily basis, were in a position to see when children had troubles at home. Some children would be upset in the classroom. On occasion a child would ask the teacher if they could stay and sleep in the school overnight. The teachers would talk to Sr. Maria, who would talk with the parents or whatever family the child had. Often the children had been left with an elderly grandparent, as the parents were gone for work reasons or in jail for drugs or drinking. At times the parent had just given up the grinding struggle of slum life and was gone, leaving the child with an auntie or uncle, possibly in an abusive situation.

Giving shelter to these children at risk quickly became an important second program for Mercy. Space was found in the slum for a Mercy home for the children, and some slum moms were brought in to work as house moms to oversee them. This was the first time some of the kids could count on getting breakfast and dinner. The shelter came to be called the "Mercy Home" program. The goal was always to eventually move the children to a good family setting if responsible relatives could be found, but to look after them and educate them if that wasn't possible. The children at the home were the Mercy kids, and that's how they are called today. The numbers grew over the years to over 200 at times. All of the children were looked after, all were educated, all were fed and, most importantly, all were loved by the house moms and staff.

After working with the sometimes broken families of the schoolchildren, Mercy workers came to see that dealing with family problems to stabilize home situations was a worthwhile goal. Sometimes what was needed was medical help, sometimes aid finding work, sometimes roof repair, sometimes full reconstruction after a slum fire. Meeting all of these needs would be part of the Mercy Community Aid program, which started in the 1980s and grew over the years.

These three programs—education, shelter, and community assistance—form the core of Mercy programs today. These programs grew over the years, and at times, such as after the tsunami in 2004, they spread to other areas of Thailand in emergency need of the community reconstruction skills of the Mercy staff.

A fourth program has been the award-winning HIV/AIDS medical shelter and hospice. Mercy developed it in the early 1990s as a response to the AIDS epidemic that enveloped Thailand in the 1980s. This epidemic soon reached the slums, where the population lacked any understanding of its origin and dangers. Mercy could not look away from this community need. Indeed, many times, severely ill patients were dropped at Mercy's door.

The following is my attempt to bring to life the programs that Mercy undertook to save the poorest of children, the magnificent people who give their lives to the children, and most important of all, the heroic children of Mercy, the Mercy kids.

Some notes on titles and names:

Throughout the following stories I will be mixing and matching Thai titles and names and nicknames. Thus it seems in order that I provide some insight on my use of these in advance.

First, Fr. Joe. Yes, he is Fr. Joe, but we spent fourteen years working together and have remained friends since. I sometimes call him Fr. Joe and sometimes Joe. That is just the way it was and is. He can handle it. What he couldn't handle is when young volunteers would take the liberty of calling him Joe without the prefix "Father." We had one twentysomething Canadian volunteer who was part of a group called

Teachers Without Borders. He didn't speak Thai, which limited his usefulness at Mercy. Mercy had and has today the best possible teachers we could have in the slum mom teachers. They understand the kids and their family situations.

One day the young volunteer, possibly stressing to Fr. Joe his teaching importance to Mercy, called him "Joe".

Explosion. "No! You, kid, cannot call me that."

The offending lad was dismissed with a brisk wave. Joe, still red in the face, spoke to me immediately after and said, "I'm Fr. Joe, you can call me 'Joe' but that punk kid can't."

Though he was popular with the younger Thai female staff, the boy disappeared soon after. Presumably somewhere, there were other brown-skinned teachers, older than himself, he could educate.

The common and polite Thai usage is to speak to people your age or older with the address *Khun* before their name, regardless of sex. That is just polite. I was usually addressed as *Khun Tom* for *Mr. Tom*. A teacher would be addressed as *Kru,* a higher-level teacher as *Ajarn.* I was sometime addressed as Kru Tom by those to whom I was teaching English, and sometimes as Leung (uncle) Tom by the kids. The latter title was, of course, my favorite form of address.

Children or those much younger are often addressed or referred to by adults as *Nong* to denote their youth. An example is the story further on of Nong Yao, not a child but much, much younger than me. In addition to the above, there is also the Thai custom of assigning nicknames to children at birth. It was explained to me that this came from the ancient Chinese belief that ghosts might attend the birth and want to steal the child. Thus, in addition to the proper name given to the child, the parents would call the child another name to confuse the ghosts. The play names could be anything unrelated to the real name, such as *frog, small, white, pineapple, fish,* or *angel.* Every Thai has a nickname. I understand the King's nickname, which is never used in public, is Lek, one of the many nicknames meaning *small.*

There is much more involved in terms of address, but the point is that courtesy in all things, starting with the titles given people, is an essential aspect of Thai culture. It's very much due, I believe, to the strong base of the Buddhist religion in Thailand. Thailand is a nonconfrontational country. Displaying respect when dealing with people is very important. No one wants to be embarrassed. The standard of conduct in this area is very high compared to the Western world and virtually all foreigners new to Thailand fail the test and end up angering the Thai they are dealing with. Of course, as part of the subdued nature of the Thai personality, no anger is shown. But the slight is not soon forgotten, if ever.

Chapter One

MEETING MERCY—1998

She screamed out, the sound breaking into the quiet air of the AIDS hospice. The young Thai medical student and I weren't prepared at all. He was only temporary help and had mentioned he would be returning to medical school the next day. The woman patient lying in the hospice bed next to us had suddenly burst out begging.

"No, don't leave me. Please don't leave me. I need you." She was on the verge of hysteria. She leaned out of the bed and grabbed at him, holding him around his legs.

I dropped down beside the bed and reached out to take her hands away from the shocked student. In an attempt to calm her, I told her, "Don't worry. I'll be here." It was my third month at Mercy and I had no idea of the power my words would have over the patient and me. On the first day I came to see if I could volunteer, I couldn't have foreseen that the path I was embarking on would bring me to that point.

Three months earlier, my first ride into the Jet Sip Rai slum was an eye-opener. The road I was on was dirty, it was desolate, and even though it was early morning, it was very hot. A Mercy driver was taking me through a major Bangkok slum. It wasn't the bright, shiny, Bangkok business districts I was used to.

I had been feeling optimistic earlier that morning. The way one does when exploring new opportunities. However, your spirit couldn't help but sag when confronted with the concrete basins, the tin-roofed shack houses squeezed together, the potholed streets, the trash on the ground that comprised the slaughterhouse district. The sun was shining, but it was a somber visage.

We rode past the dismal concrete, rusted metal, and grayness of the early morning slaughterhouse pit. Crows, strutting and pecking at specks of pig flesh left over from the previous night's work, rustled into the air as we bumped by. Seconds later, I was dropped on the edge of the dirt road as it approached the river and directed to a rickety plank walkway on wooden pilings. All of the pilings appeared as if they would fall into the murky, garbage-strewn water underneath with just a nudge. It was March, the beginning of the very hot season in Thailand. The morning air was already steamy. My shirt was wet, sticking to me. My sunglasses were fogging up. I was on my way to meet Fr. Joe Maier at his home in the slum near here.

I had called Mercy for an appointment the previous afternoon. The person who took the call and invited me to come down the next day was Tim Hague. Tim was a Canadian in his late fifties who had worked in the hotel business in Bangkok. He had been with Mercy for several years. His responsibility at Mercy was keeping the books, but in the coming months, he would also come to be a source of advice for me on how Mercy worked. Much of that advice came in the form of warnings about staffers who had areas of responsibility, and whose sensitivities I would have to be aware of. It was my first lesson. Even in a charitable organization, there were turf issues that had to be handled with care.

On the morning I was to meet with Joe, it wasn't to be at the small office he had in a rundown old warehouse-style building on Soi 40 off Rama 4 Road, the main street that runs outside of the slum area. Despite its condition, the warehouse was on the "right side of the rail tracks," as one might say. When I reached the warehouse office, Tim told me that Joe would meet me in the shack he called home, down in the slaughterhouse and slum area, close to the intersection of the Phra Khanong canal and the Chao Phraya river. A Mercy driver took me over, and the short journey was an education. Perhaps that was why Joe had decided I should take it, or perhaps it just fit his schedule for the day.

The entire area of the Mercy Centre, of the Jet Sip Rai slum in which it's located, of the slaughterhouse and the tattered apartment blocks in the area, is all on land owned by the Port Authority of Thailand. All residing therein are squatters. All are part of a community of the poorest who came from the Thai countryside to the Bangkok area after World War II and then again during the Vietnam War as the port grew rapidly in response to heavy wartime traffic. Stevedore jobs were available. The sure money to be made working as a stevedore at the port was not much, but it was safer than the annual gamble of farming in the countryside.

The greatest part of the port authority property was basically swampland between the river and the cargo rail line running parallel to the river. This land was unused by the port authority and thus available for poor folks to squat on. Squatting on unused property has some legal protection in Thailand. That provided the basis for the thousands of people who flooded into the open lands of the port authority after the wars. Rough wooden shacks with tin roofs were built. There was no running water, no legal electricity, and minimal plumbing leading into open sewers running through the housing blocks. It was primitive, but it was a no-cost place to sleep sheltered from the elements.

Most of the members of Joe's parish were slaughterhouse workers. This is the part of the slum where the animals, mostly pigs but some cattle, were killed. They were hit over the head with metal pipes, then cut up and delivered to the fresh markets early every morning. As Buddhism prohibits the killing of all living things and Muslims avoid pork, the work was left to the poor Catholic community. These were, for the most part, people of Vietnamese background who had come to Thailand and then Bangkok more than fifty years before to escape the wars in Indochina. Thus, Fr. Joe's church was known as the slaughterhouse parish and he was known as the slaughterhouse priest.

Joe believed working with the poor meant living with the poor. He had left the Redemptorist priest's house in central Bangkok in 1981. His residence was one of a number of shacks built on stilts out over the watery margins of the intersection of the canal and the river.

As the driver departed, I surveyed the collection of precariously perched wooden hovels scattered along the river waterfront. I hesitantly stepped on the worn plank walkway and went past several shacks. Careful steps. Eyes down. Balancing. The walkway jogged to the left past a few more shacks. Finally, I saw a Thai lady, who I presumed was a staffer working for Mercy. She was standing outside Joe's shack, waving me on in.

This was 1998. I should note that Joe would live in this shack for over twenty years after moving in, from 1981 until about 2001. At that time, a donor offering to finance new buildings for the Mercy Centre would insist that as part of the deal, Joe move into a new residence on the Mercy grounds.

Inside, I was shown a place to sit. The light was dim. Besides the open doorway, there was only a small square of a window frame. It had no glass, but a wooden rain cover propped open by a stick allowed air flow. There was a small lamp on a side table. In a corner shrine, the Virgin Mary looked down benevolently, hands at her side, palms extended outward, giving a benediction, I thought. The wooden planks that comprised the floor had a linoleum covering, curling somewhat at the edges. A fan circulated a desultory breeze against the early morning heat. The staff lady called out and then, from behind a curtain of wooden beads, Joe pushed through from a side room (his bedroom, I guessed) and greeted me. I was later to learn that his bed was a simple cot.

I can't remember the details of the conversation. I gave a bit of my business background and my Catholic education. I repeated my wish to be allowed to volunteer. I do remember saying that I wasn't sure what I could do that would be useful at first, but I was open to whatever was needed.

Joe was very gracious. I didn't know what he thought, as Joe was quite Thai in being able to mask his thinking unless somebody really irritated him. What he said, however, was clear.

"Don't worry about where you might fit in. Come. Be a tourist. Things will develop." I thought that was the best invitation I could get.

When Joe spoke of the organization of Mercy, he did cause some warning bells to go off when he told me the organization was quite simple. They were organized much like a Chinese family, of which he was the father. My business training would say that was a terrible management model with little responsibility or recognition given to others in the family. However, wisely I think, I kept my mouth shut. I learned that Joe would stick to that model throughout the years no matter how many friends, donors, or supporters would suggest to him that a more open style of management would help Mercy grow better.

My main takeaways from that meeting were the open invitation and my impression that Mercy would be on the front lines of working with the poor and their children. The grimness of slum living was a shock, but I told myself that I had survived grim conditions as a combat infantry officer in Vietnam years before. I could handle this.

Volunteers coming to a street-based organization that works with children will find themselves very much the outsiders, especially if they have no professional background in social work. You are an amateur coming to work with the pros. The distance from the local professional staff is more than doubled when the volunteer is from a foreign country and has limited knowledge of the local language and customs. Though I had worked in Thailand for several years, this was the situation I found myself in as an American businessman, coming into the very close family of social workers that comprised the Mercy staff.

As I reported to the warehouse office in the following days, I learned just being a tourist would be difficult. Mercy was its own puzzle. The Soi 40 warehouse office was removed from the actual Mercy Centre, which was in the middle of the Jet Sip Rai slum, a five minutes' drive away across the rail tracks. Besides the small office space for Fr. Joe and an open area for Tim Hague and a Thai secretary, there were forty girls, from three to fifteen years old, under the care of Mercy, residing in open bunk bed arrangements on the second floor. They were looked after by a thirtyish house mom, Jai, who was married to a Thai army officer. There was a cook on the staff, a very rotund and cheerful lady with two children, to fix the meals in the morning and evening. I quickly learned that Jai was magic as a house mom. She provided the girls the understanding, counseling, and direction they needed. Jai would become a great friend. She spoke very good English and was the one who enabled me to get a grip on how I could be of use to Mercy. We are still friends today.

Jai had two bright, energetic young girls in their early twenties as assistants to help manage the house. Their names were Kung and Dtim. They had been sent down to Mercy from Nong Kai, a village on the Mekong River in the very northernmost area of Thailand. A fellow Redemptorist priest and good friend of Fr. Joe's, Fr. Mike Shea, had founded the Sarnelli House for orphans in Nong Khai. Fr. Joe and Fr. Mike had studied together in the Redemptorist seminary in Oconomowoc, Wisconsin and had come to Thailand at the same time. I believe it was felt the girls would gain experience at Mercy and then return to the Sarnelli House to take up larger roles there.

During the day, the Mercy girls went to public schools. One of the house rules was that the girls were all assigned chores to help with the cooking and serving of the meals as well as the housecleaning. When they started coming home from school it was a maelstrom of noise: girls talking, girls yelling, girls laughing. Some brave girls would come over to stand behind Jai as she and I talked so they could examine the new foreigner.

Thus, the Soi 40 house became my base. From here would begin my exploration of Mercy, and of my fitness to serve.

As most volunteers did, I fell in love with all the Mercy kids. But it had become clear to me at the very start that Mercy had excellent counselors who shared the kids' language and religion. They understood them and could help them much better than I ever could. I came to know the faces and greet as many of the kids as possible. Virtually 200 or more kids were in the Mercy homes program at any time, so I was unable to know most of them in any depth. Of course, there were some exceptions for both the Mercy staff and volunteers. Here, and posted after the following chapters, are some of the kids and their stories.

Sai—The Teddy Bear Girl

Seven-year-old Sai and her younger brother were brought to the girl's home on Soi 40 by concerned neighbors one evening. The neighbors found them alone in their shack in the slum. It seems that their parents had been arrested and taken off to jail earlier in the day for some drug offense. The children had no one else to turn to and nowhere else to go. Familiar with Mercy's work over the past thirty years in the port area of Bangkok, the neighbors thought Mercy might take these two children in.

The staff managed to find a bed for them up on the second floor, and the two children got settled in that night. The next morning, all the other children headed off to school, but no arrangements had yet been made to get Sai and her brother into some local primary school. For that day at least, they were just going to have to stay there and explore their new home.

One thing Sai noticed about this new place is that everyone seemed so rich! There were stuffed toys on all the beds. Everyone seemed to have so much! What place had she landed in? And how long before she would be taken out of here and off to somewhere else? In her young mind, she felt she had to take some control over her future while the staff busied themselves with their morning chores. About an hour later, sensing that unnatural quiet that always tells parents something is up, one of the staff located Sai outside the entrance. She had taken as many of the stuffed toys as she could carry down the stairs and set up shop on the sidewalk to sell them.

This first episode showed that the young girl had what one of the volunteers, a Canadian lady named Mary McLean, would call *grit*. Mary would tutor Sai in English and seventh-grade studies for a possible home/study opportunity in the U.S. Unfortunately, that opportunity fell through. Sai had studied hard and was quite disappointed, but she wouldn't be stopped. Mary knew she was determined to get ahead.

Sai did well in Mercy and graduated from high school. It would seem her early inclination to the sales world would become her commercial path. Today she is working in a woman's clothing outlet, the Platinum Mall, in Bangkok. Twice a year, she returns to Mercy with clothing for the Mercy girls.

Credit to volunteers Graeme Bristol
and Mary McLean.

Vietnam—September 1966—First Lesson

The day was to start with an air assault. It was my first. The sun had been up over an hour, but the heat of the day had not yet hit as we filed out of the base camp to a dirt road in a nearby open area. We were lined up in groups of six along the dirt road that would serve as the pickup zone, six being the number of combat-laden American soldiers a Huey slick ship or transport chopper could carry in the tropical heat.

While we were waiting, one of the young sergeants, Bobby Woods, a six-foot-tall avid skier from New York who'd become a ski trooper in Alaska, came to me and gave me some advice on boarding the chopper. There are four web seats against the back hull in the Huey chopper we used in Vietnam, the other troopers sit on the floor. Woods told me, "Sir, when you get on, sit in one of the middle seats. It'll be safer there."

I thanked him but told him I wouldn't. Of course, he was right. The guys on either side of that seat were more likely to catch a bullet than me if we went into a hot LZ. Such selfishness, however, is not the way to show you are ready to lead men into combat. I could see Woods was genuinely concerned. He didn't want to lose his new platoon leader so quickly after he arrived in Vietnam.

When the choppers came in to pick us up, I got aboard last and sat on the floor. We had four soldiers on the web seats, and I was back-to-back with another soldier facing the open doors. From this position, I could see everything unfold as we came in and could be the first to jump down when the chopper reached the LZ.

Aerial assaults always start with your stomach curdling as the chopper pitches and rolls in the air wake of the gunships leading the assault and prepping the site. You wait to see if the LZ is hot or not. Here, it was not. There were only a few shots taken at us on landing, and whoever had taken them disappeared as we unloaded from the choppers. A village on the intersection of a river and a major canal would be the end objective after seven to eight hours of walking and checking what we might find along the way.

We started the long, hot walk toward our objective. We soon stepped out of the rice paddies onto narrow footpaths that weaved through coconut palms, bamboo growth, and scrub brush. Even though we were in the shade, there was no breeze, and the temperature was around ninety-five degrees. The jungle is an oppressive force. *National Geographic* would have us believe it is continuously creating new life, but the opposite is equally true. The jungle is constantly dying and rotting. We could smell it in the humid, sweltering air; we could feel its corruption on our sweat-soaked skin as we slowly made our way along the footpath.

It took eight hours to reach our objective. We had moved slowly, carefully, checking out the surrounding areas as we went. I had expected a change of atmosphere when we closed on the abandoned village but not such a fetid change. The huts, with their mud floors, rotting bamboo walls, and collapsing thatched straw roofs, were clearly long abandoned. Possibly due to the many floods and deposits of primeval river-bottom mud, they retained the stench of putrefaction.

The village lay at the intersection of a river and a large canal. A smaller canal ran through it, with footpaths on either side where the huts were clustered. There was little room to spare between the smaller canal and the wetland and bamboo growth at the edge of the forest, which pressed right up against the village huts. The village lay dank and dark as the shadows of the approaching night loomed over us.

When we arrived, it was late afternoon. I was told to call in the squad from my platoon, who had been put on a stay-behind ambush. They came in about twenty minutes later and joined the troops lying along both sides of the two footpaths that went through the village. The mud and bamboo huts were located along the footpaths. The footpath my platoon came in on was away from the river and nearer the forest. As my platoon was the last to come into the village, there was only one hut, nearest the thick stand of bamboo separating the village from the forest, left unoccupied. I entered the hut and saw no furniture apart from a couple of wooden stools and a rough wooden platform three feet off the ground, which a Westerner might take for a dining table, but which served as a bed in Vietnam. I sat down on it, dropped my backpack, and told my radiotelephone operator (RTO) to put his equipment on it to make sure it would stay dry. As I looked around, I was satisfied that at least we wouldn't be sleeping in the mud that night.

Having taken that short break, I knew I had to see to the placement of my platoon and find out if we had any specific orders for the night. I left the hut and found my platoon sergeant, Sergeant Amado, on one knee alongside the footpath, checking on how the platoon was arranged. He told me the stay-behind squad was back inside the company perimeter. I had just started to talk to him about how best to cover the way we had come in when it started.

We received a burst of automatic weapons and small-arms fire, not from the direction of our entry route, but very close by, on the other side of the bamboo growth behind the adjacent huts. It was my first time under fire. I had the silly thought, *It's just like they say, with the sound of the bullets whizzing past your head like a bee flying by at high speed.* Since I was already bent down on one knee and leaning over to talk with Sergeant Amado, it was easy to hit the ground. At first, we weren't sure of the direction of fire, so the troops opened up in response pretty much along the way we had come in, but off to the side a bit at the area thicker with bushes and bamboo.

After a few minutes, the incoming fire stopped, and we received orders from the battalion commanding officer to cease fire. We checked with our squad leaders to see if we had casualties and found no one had been hit. I was told to send a squad back up the trail, opening fire and pushing toward where we thought the enemy shooting had come from. We did, but there was no response. The Viet Cong had either followed us and gone to the jungle-covered side of the village to take us under fire or, as I came later to think was more probable, had anticipated where we were going and waited on the other side of the bamboo for all the troops to place themselves in the village before they opened up. After firing a magazine or two, they had taken off.

All the reconnaissance had finished, and we were set for the night, having put a listening post in place fifty meters outside the perimeter. I had had my introduction to enemy fire and the abrupt possibility of death it had presented. But when I walked back into the hut, I got my second major shock of the day.

The bamboo wall of the hut, right behind the wooden platform I had been sitting on for a minute or two, had a long string of holes running left to right about a foot above its level. If I had remained sitting there, instead of kneeling out on the trail in front of the hut, at least two of those rounds would have pierced my chest. For me, it was just like the movies. It could have been a *Rambo* movie with the line of machine gun bullets stitched along the wall. Only this was real, and it was a wall *I* had been sitting against.

Of course, the VC were out to kill as many Americans as possible, not just me. It was just chance that I had sat there in the hut talking to my RTO for a few seconds while the VC were on the other side of the bamboo thicket. I was sure they had heard our voices, so when they opened fire, that had seemed to them a good direction in which to shoot.

I thought later that the reason we had all escaped injury was very simple. The VC who had shot at us, maybe only five or six men with a couple of AK-47s, had been standing up, unable to see through the bamboo. They would have held their weapons above waist height, tight and close to their chests, to steady the automatic fire. As a result, the rounds went high because the American soldiers were all lying or sitting down on the ground after hours of tough, hot walking through thick brush. The bullets went over our heads.

However, I now clearly understood the message. They. Had. Meant. To. Kill. Me. It left an impression. That was my first lesson. Now I understood what war was all about for the guys on the ground. It was about killing. Killing and surviving. Nothing else.

A sad end to this story is that Sgt. Bobby Woods, who had tried to guide me to safety, was KIA in an air assault in early January. He was sitting in the end seat he had advised me against and was hit in the side by a bullet before he could get off the chopper. He fell to the floor. The chopper crew immediately flew him to an Army hospital, but he had gone into shock and was dead on arrival. He was young, twenty-three I believe, and full of spirit. He had been an avid skier who joined the army asking to be assigned to the winter soldiers, the 9th Infantry Regiment, then in Alaska. But he found himself traveling along with the 9th Infantry to Hawaii, and then on to Vietnam as the U.S. army mobilized for the war. The guys in the platoon loved him, as did I. Sgt. Amado and I were both in tears after he died.

Chapter Two

NONG YAO—1998

At the time I started with Mercy, in March 1998, there was a twenty-one-year-old American woman, Beth, who was living at the Soi 40 house and working as a volunteer with Mercy. She was from Iowa and had met Fr. Joe when he gave a talk at her church the previous fall. She had asked Fr. Joe if he would accept her and her boyfriend as volunteers. He said yes, and she decided to take a break from school and come to Thailand after the new year.

She was slender, had long blond hair, and was enormously popular with the Soi 40 girls. To the girls, she seemed like a movie star who had come to stay with them.

Unfortunately for her boyfriend, he couldn't stay at the Soi 40 house with the girls. He had a small, somewhat rundown room and bed at the main Mercy building where about eighty boys stayed. That was in bloc six (the Thai use "bloc" instead of "block") of the Jet Sip Rai slum, closer to the port, which was where he took his meals. Their opportunities to be together were very limited, and he was not a happy camper. Apparently, it had not been his idea to volunteer, but love knows no bounds. After three months, he had learned a little of the language and was able to help on a limited basis as a handyman.

Beth, an ardent Catholic, was looking to serve with a capital S, and she had decided to work at the AIDS hospice. She assisted the nurses as she could and gave massages to the bed-bound AIDS patients.

In deciding where to start to gain a look into Mercy, I decided to follow Beth's lead and went to investigate the HIV/AIDS program. My experience there would give me a quick and harsh introduction to the desperate lives the poor lead, whether in the slums of Bangkok, elsewhere in Thailand, or elsewhere in the world.

I went over to the main Mercy Centre building in the Jet Sip Rai slum. At that time, that was a two-story building of cement block, painted yellow. It had offices and a small open-sided one-room preschool, built around a gravel courtyard where vehicles could park. The Hospice was in a wing on the left side of the building as you entered, a couple of steps up from the street.

I had no plan except to introduce myself, meet the staff, and observe to learn the mechanics of the hospice. While I greatly respected what Beth was doing, I wasn't sure I would be any good at giving massages. I asked to meet the person in charge and was introduced to Khun Usanee. Usanee, who had trained in the U.K., was the head nurse and manager. There were several nurses on the staff but no doctors. Some doctors from a nearby government hospital came through periodically or were on call if Usanee felt she and the hospice staff needed medical advice.

Mercy had recruited Khun Usanee five years earlier to be the founding staff member of the hospice and the AIDS program. She was a working mom and devoted to her work. She also became a close friend who enabled me to function in a useful manner at Mercy. She is still a friend today. Eight years after we met, she would be appointed the executive director of Mercy, although that was only to the extent that Fr. Joe would let anyone else have a say in things. She has been a key person in Mercy's success going forward.

That morning was an important lesson in how Mercy functioned for volunteers. Jumping into the deep end of the pool was allowed for anyone foolish enough to do so. At that time, they had about thirty beds in the hospice wing; however, they were all full. A few people were lying on extra beds set up near the entrance to the ward. It was next to one of those extra beds where the Thai intern told me of his plans to leave and upset the woman patient as I mentioned earlier. I had promised to come and visit her the next day.

When I returned the next day in the early afternoon. I found the bed in the overflow area empty and asked one of the nurses about the woman who had been there. The nurse, named Mos, told me she had been moved inside the hospice proper. Pausing to see I washed my hands, he guided me into where she was lying.

I had glimpsed the interior of the ward on the previous visit but had not gone in. Now it became real. It was a bare-bones slum hospice. Cement floor. High unfinished ceiling. No air conditioning. Open windows and doors with mosquito screens. Standing fans, trying to provide some cooling effect, really just stirring the hot air. No dividers between beds. Air circulation was an important protection against tuberculosis. I was to learn that most of the patients, their immune systems compromised, would eventually die of TB. Cement toilet stalls were on one side and shower stalls were next to them. Strong odors. Medicine. Very quiet. Skeletal patients with no strength to speak up or act up. Looking at death. Withdrawn. Withdrawing.

As we walked toward the part of the ward set aside for women, Mos asked me to encourage the patient to eat and exercise when I spoke with her. Apparently, she was resisting getting out of bed due to the pain it caused in her joints. She was wearing diapers under her hospital gown, as were most of the other patients.

At this time, AIDS was spreading widely among younger people in Thailand. In the early nineties, it had been considered a disease for homosexual men. As the years had gone by, however, it had spread into the night scene overall, with many women becoming infected and then infecting men with whom they had sexual relations. It was made worse by the lack of treatment, due to the stigma attached to the disease, which condemned many to death. Private hospitals would not accept AIDS patients for fear of scaring away other patients. There were severe limitations on the medicines available. It was not unknown for doctors at government hospitals to tell a prospective patient that it would be best to go home and die with their family.

The families of those infected were ashamed, feeling they had lost face. They didn't want it known in the community that their son or daughter had the disease. Most often, when the infected person went home, the family would hide them in a back room and try to treat them with traditional medicines. Thus, when a patient came to Mercy for treatment, they were advanced cases, often virtual skeletons. For many, almost all, it was too late. No combination of medicine or care could save them. The medicines were free to Mercy from the government; however, as a visiting nurse from the U.S. told me, the medicines available in Thailand were five years or more behind those being used in the U.S.

Her name was Nong Yao. She was in her late twenties or early thirties. Her face and body were so marked by the disease that I couldn't make any judgment as to how she might appear when healthy. I spent an hour with her. We talked; her English was fairly good. My limited Thai helped. She told me she had worked in Japan for a few years. She made no mention of what job she had done there. She had pain in her calves and feet and asked me to massage them, and I did. There were eight other beds around us, women in their thirties and forties. Some of the women patients watched us as an object of curiosity; most were just too listless to care.

When it came time for me to go, Nong Yao became agitated and made me promise that I would come again the next day. I said I would. Then she asked me, "What about the day after that?" I stopped to consider what I was getting myself into. She grabbed my arm and I could see the panic in her eyes. I told her that I would come to visit every day until she got well, but she needed to work to get well. She relaxed. She had heard me say that I would return but possibly not the part about working to get well.

As I was leaving, nurse Mos caught up with me and reminded me to wash my hands with disinfectant soap. AIDS patients are often victim to a variety of skin diseases as part of their failing immunity system. "Wash before you go in. Wash when you are leaving. Wash as many times during the day as you think of it."

I washed and washed again. I learned that Beth, the young American volunteer, had picked up some bad skin rashes over the prior few months. While the rashes had been treated, the lesson was clear; if you were in contact with a patient, wash, wash and wash again.

That was in mid-May, the hottest season in Thailand until the June rains came and cooled things off. Daily temperatures reached the mid-nineties and higher with matching humidity. I continued to return, almost every day, though I would take Sundays off. The nurse enlisted me to assist in getting Nong Yao to stand up and take a few steps. She was crying and begging to stop. She said it hurt too much, but the nurse said it was necessary to get her started moving again. Tough love. We did the procedure every day I visited, and within a week, she was walking unassisted. Then, with the assistance of one of the female staff, she was able to go to the bathroom and wash up in the shower. It was a celebration. No more diapers.

She was still very thin but had recovered some strength. I told her I would be taking some days off. She wasn't happy, but the process was wearing me down emotionally even though it was only an hour or two a day. I concluded that I needed to pace myself.

We talked more day by day. Nong Yao was a farm girl from the far North of Thailand. Her home was in the village area called Pai.

We talked for weeks. I was doing other small chores at Mercy but always found time to stop in. Late morning became my preferred time, as I could easily leave as we broke for lunch. Nong Yao was no longer getting her food served to her in bed. Once she started walking, the nurses insisted she walk to the hospice lunch table to join others to eat. She resisted, saying she wasn't strong enough. The nurses told her; no walk, no eat. She walked. More tough love.

We talked. Nong Yao walked. I massaged. I learned she had a British boyfriend. He remained at their apartment and was also very sick with AIDS. He refused to come into the hospice.

She was getting stronger but was still very thin and limited when walking. One day, as I was about to leave, she grabbed my arm again. A familiar restraining gesture by then. She was very intense this day, pulling me toward her.

She asked me, "Do you love me?"

I understood the love she was seeking was not what I intended. At the same time, her intensity and desperation deserved an answer. I was stopped in my tracks and paused a moment or two.

Then I leaned toward her lying in her hospice bed and said, "God loves you and I love you too."

Right or wrong, I don't know. She seemed to accept it and let go of my arm.

That was a Friday. I was exhausted from the week, from the heat, from the utter reality of Mercy. I decided to take two days off.

After my introduction to death thirty years earlier in my first days in Vietnam, I thought I had left death behind. In coming to Mercy, I hadn't anticipated that a reintroduction to death was to be a part of the world I entered. For the poorest of people in the slums, death is a frequent visitor. Fr. Joe had described Mercy's work in the slums as combat. It was a different kind of war, but I was to learn that the term did indeed reflect the reality of Mercy.

When I came in on Monday, I found Nong Yao's bed in the hospice filled by another patient. I asked Mos what had happened. He told me that Nong Yao's parents had come from the North of Thailand to take her home on Sunday morning. Fr. Joe had come by after mass and signed some papers releasing her to her parents and they had gone.

I was stunned. I would have liked a chance to say goodbye. Fr. Joe and I had casually spoken together several times during the weeks I had visited with Nong Yao. He knew she was a patient I had invested time and effort with, but he didn't give me the courtesy of a phone call to let me know what was happening.

At first, I was a bit angry and felt a sense of loss, but then it hit me. I had no right to be upset. I was an amateur and had acted as an amateur. I now learned an important lesson that the professional medical people who worked these situations all knew. Care for the patients, but keep a professional distance.

Nong Yao was now home with her parents on the farm. No doubt she would die there in a matter of months. The medicine, the disciplined care she needed, wouldn't be available. I don't know if her parents realized that, but maybe they did. Maybe the decision was for Nong Yao to die at home. God bless them. It would be a very difficult time for the family.

I felt an enormous sense of loss. I wouldn't work in the hospice again. I would visit and care but keep my distance emotionally.

To me, the nurses are all heroes. I owe a debt of thanks to Mos, the gentle male nurse, who took the time to educate me on how to function in a medical setting.

Except, years later, I would forget that rule of keeping my distance and pay the price again.

The Follow-Me-Home Girl, Em

Early on at Mercy, I was almost a daily visitor to the girls' house on Soi 40. I would touch base with both Jai and Tim Hague. They would help me interpret whatever Mercy doings I had been involved in that day. It was a pleasure to be there when the kids came home from school. It was just a joyous mess of giggles and screams that made you feel younger and happier just to be there.

During that time, at the Soi 40 house, an event took place that would foreshadow my commitment and time at Mercy. Jai had organized a party, a going-home event for Beth the young volunteer, whose work in the AIDS ward had led me into volunteering there. Beth and her boyfriend were leaving. The Soi 40 girls were devastated. They all, in some way, had lost the people they had loved and who had loved them previously in life. Beth had been at Mercy, living with them, sharing their meals, every day for over six months. I had stopped by after work to say my goodbyes to Beth. As I came into the house, there was a ring of kids around her and a lot of crying going on. She was an impressive and spiritually strong young lady. She told me she would continue to volunteer after she had a chance to rest at home in Iowa. She was thinking she would work with a Catholic aid group in Sudan. Amazing woman.

Before I could leave, I felt one of the Soi 40 girls, Em, tugging at my hand. She had been crying but now looked up to me, speaking in Thai, "Beth's leaving us, Uncle Tom. You're not going to leave, are you, Uncle Tom? You'll stay with us?"

Wow. My mind flashed back to my experience with Nong Yao at the AIDS ward. What was I to do? My response, again, was instantaneous, not thought out in any sense. I knelt down next to Em and told her, "No, Em, I'm not leaving. I'll be here." She just smiled, nodded her head, and went back to join the other girls around Beth.

As I went on home a few minutes later, I thought about what I had said. When I had come to Mercy, I hadn't had a timeframe in mind. I just wanted to learn what Mercy was and try to be of use. No plan or thought beyond that, though I guess I had it in mind to go back to the business world at some point. Was I now committed to Mercy indefinitely? Not at that moment, but the moment with Nan and her request would influence my coming to a commitment. It was the kids that would keep me there, that year and all the years to follow.

In the weeks that followed, Em would always come to say hi to me when I came by Soi 40 after the kids came home from school, but she was just checking that I was there, not clinging at all. I came to look forward to the ritual. One day, though, as I went out the door to walk down the alleyway to the main street to catch a taxi, I looked back, and Em had followed me. She was about twenty feet behind me and just walking with me, not trying to catch up. I waved to her and motioned for her to go back inside the house. She waved back but didn't move. I turned around and kept walking. I looked back after a few steps and Em was walking along again, following me. We repeated the waves and the gesture to go back. As I neared the street, I looked back again, and she had returned to the house. We did this exchange of good-bye waves several times in the following weeks.

There would be an ending that would repeat the lesson I should have learned with Nong Yao. One may commit to Mercy, but the reality of Mercy wouldn't have any respect for that commitment. Mercy's work protecting children evolved in its own way. One day, I came back to Soi 40 and noticed Em was not around. I asked Jai about it. She told me that they had found some relatives and Em had gone to be with them.

Mercy is not an orphanage. Many of the kids had relatives if they could just be found, though in the end, a safe home could not be found for many. The rule of sending the children home to a relative extended to any safe home, no matter how poor. It was Fr. Joe's and Sr. Maria's position, and a correct one I believe, that if a relative was found, an auntie or uncle who would take the child and care for them, that was where they belonged. He included the poorest of homes in that idea. He would enjoy, at times, exposing some visitor to that vision. "No matter how derelict the shack. Even if there are holes in the roof, rats and roaches running around, if it's family, that child belongs in a home with that family." This vision of a possible home in poverty horrified many Western donors and visitors, but of course, the child wasn't abandoned. Mercy still had a responsibility. The community staff would still look in on the family. If the roof had holes in it, the staff would find a way to fix it. What help the family home needed to be a better place, Mercy would give.

It was a victory for Mercy and the best solution for Em, but once again, it did sting. I was thrown a bit off balance. I had to learn to be professional, to engage, but at the same time, to keep some distance. Someday. Maybe.

Chapter Three

TRY TO BE USEFUL—1998

M y experience with Nong Yao was to trigger some in-depth thought on my part as to what would be an appropriate mindset and role for myself and other volunteers.

Fr. Joe is always the gatekeeper for Mercy volunteers. They approach him after he preaches in churches on his travels to the U.S. or Canada or through friends or donors. Years later, I would be given the responsibility of vetting volunteers and guiding them to Mercy. One of the most important guidelines I could give volunteers after their arrival was simple but at the same time, very difficult for many.

The advice was, "You have to change for Mercy. Mercy will not change for you."

What I meant was, if they wanted to contribute and not just be a visitor, they had to find ways that they could fit in. Language was a problem. Few of the staff spoke English. Even today, some of the senior managers don't. Most volunteers were at Mercy for a short stay, usually anywhere from two weeks to a month, not really enough time to pick up any useful Thai language ability. If I could suggest something for these volunteers to do, I would, but that was often not the case. Many of the newly arrived volunteers would be frustrated that no one was coming to them to show their appreciation of them for volunteering. No one was coming to say, "Join my team."

I remember a very nice lady, a piano teacher, who came from the U.K. to volunteer, thinking she would teach piano to some of the kids. All very good, except we had no piano and, at that time, no real music program.

Her arrival was a surprise to me. No one she had communicated with prior to her arrival had mentioned possible issues with the music program. If she would be doing something, it would have to be ad hoc. She was very frustrated. I could only tell her she would have to learn what Mercy was and create a space, musical in nature, if that was to be her focus. No one could help her. They were all busy with their own duties. It was up to the volunteers to learn what Mercy was, learn where they could contribute, and then, as Nike says, "Just do it."

It should be said that Fr. Joe was a part of the problem in that he usually couldn't say no. On his overseas trips when he met people and they requested to come to Mercy as a volunteer, he didn't ever want to have the unpleasant experience of saying no. This is a very Thai trait he has incorporated in himself. He would be all smiles and welcome. "Of course. Please come. We would love to have you at Mercy. You can do so much." Unfortunately, many people took him at his charming word. Not all of those who came had the time and gumption it would take to carve out a space in which they could contribute.

An experience I had in my first few months at Mercy, carving out a space to contribute, is a small example of what I would tell new volunteers. While visiting with Nong Yao at the Mercy Centre hospice, I noticed there was a square of asphalt in one corner of the courtyard and a basketball hoop. The older boys, and some of the drivers, would shoot hoops at night before dinner. As I looked it over, it hit me that something was missing. There were no lines on the court. No out-of-bounds lines. No free-throw line. No key lines, which are, of course, important if you are practicing to shoot from the top of the key. This was something I could do. So I did it.

I went on the internet to check that I would be using the proper measurements and outlined them on a pad of paper. Then I went to a supply store and brought a tape measure, duct tape, and spray paint. Early the next morning, before it got too hot, I went to the hoops court (or half-court), measured, taped, and then spray-painted the lines. No one asked me what I was doing. No one volunteered to help. That was fine. The next day I heard from some of the drivers that the boys and staff liked the new lines and were using them to plan and practice their shots.

Given the many needs of Mercy, this was a very small victory, but it felt good. I had seen the need, taken the initiative, and made a positive contribution of which I was privately proud.

About a year later, the hoops court was taken out by construction to expand the area for the new school. My effort of that day was gone, but so what? It had been a positive change I could talk about with new volunteers.

Mercy will not conform to you. You must conform to Mercy. Find something you can do to help and do it. Don't look for help. Don't look for praise. Just do it. That was not always a popular sentiment for volunteers, some of whom were convinced that just by volunteering they were adding value and doing God's work. Sorry, if you want to add value, find work of value and do it.

Commitment, especially the commitment of time, is important. The best volunteers were the ones who took the time, who were either living in Thailand or visitors planning to stay several months or more at a time. They would come to understand some Thai language, customs, and most importantly, the personality and needs of the Thai staff. In the end, we were just assisting that staff. Being dependable in your attendance and attention to Mercy is important. The staff and the kids need to know you'll be there. You can't just be a drop-in guest. I would imagine this would apply to volunteering in any social welfare organization around the world.

The Woodshop Boy—Som

Most of the families in the Jet Sip Rai slum area were Thai and from Bangkok. Additionally, over time, more poor families were moving in from the farming areas of Thailand, notably Isan in the northwest. Also, some of the teens who came were from the hill tribes, whose villages were on the mountainous border areas with Burma and Laos.

Khun Samran, the leader of the street kids outreach program, came across a hill tribe boy being held in the children's jail and arranged to have him brought into the Mercy Centre. I don't think he was in jail for any special crime. It was just that the police had found him adrift on the streets with no residence in Bangkok and thought it best to have him detained. He was a sturdy lad, about seventeen years old, and his name was Som. He was from a hill tribe in the golden triangle, the nexus of Burma, Laos, and Thailand, to the north of Chiang Rai.

When he was brought into Mercy, it was expected that Som would come into the fold at Mercy and go to school. That he did, and much more. At that time a volunteer couple was in residence: Mike and Deborah Simms, repeat volunteers for several months a year for several years. Mike, a retired fire captain, had used his skills in construction and woodwork to set up a small woodshop. In an empty shack near the Mercy Centre, he had begun teaching classes to older Mercy kids to give them confidence and a marketable trade in woodworking. In typical do-it-yourself fashion for Mercy, Mike had to do it on his own with only part-time help from one of the maintenance staff. Mike purchased all the basic equipment using his own funds and donations from friends. Each year, as he and Deborah returned, he expanded the shop with more equipment and more classes.

Som proved to have a talent for woodworking. He studied with Mike in the woodshop and, over the years, took over the manufacturing of wood products, such as benches to be used in the schools and at the Mercy Centre. When Som was ready to leave Mercy, Mike and Deborah financed his trade education in air-conditioning repair. Initially, Som went back to his family in the north, earning a living and supporting himself and his family. I later learned that he had gotten married in his home village and he and his wife had returned to work in Bangkok.

Credit to volunteers Mike and Deborah Simms.

Vietnam—October 1966—River Crossing

Death is always present. That is the essence of combat and life in a combat zone. It may come at the most unexpected moment or in the most unexpected way, but you must learn, you must carry the knowledge in your fiber, that death is always present, and you must always be on the lookout for it.

A river crossing in the field, in normal circumstances, need not be dangerous, though it requires great care. Even in combat zones, if you are not under fire or engaged with the enemy or under emergency time pressure, there need be no danger. This was such an occasion.

We were on a somewhat bizarre expedition, but those who've lived military experience will know such a thing is possible, even if not completely intelligible in the cold light of normal-world logic.

An officer's promotion in the military is dependent on the quality of the efficiency reports he receives. Why is that explanation necessary? Because, without it, it may be difficult to understand why the following escapade was even planned, much less allowed to happen.

In our company, we had a first lieutenant, an infantry officer, serving as company executive officer or XO. Let's call him Lieutenant Big, as he was six foot, two inches tall and must have weighed 225 pounds. He looked like a football lineman. Lieutenant Big was an obnoxious fellow, not liked in the company by either enlisted men or his fellow officers. Most in the military understand that rank distinctions among lieutenants are nebulous, but he was the kind of first lieutenant who insisted that second lieutenants he encountered salute him.

In my first week in the unit, as we junior officers sat talking in our hooch preparing to sack out late one night, Lieutenant Big came in and decided to haze the new officer. He ordered me to go down to the cooks' sleeping area, wake them up, and have them make him a pizza. I was incredulous; if we were back in the States I could understand some level of hazing, but not here in Vietnam. I made him repeat the order, said "Yes, sir", and then walked down to the bunker line, sat on a sand-bagged wall, and stared at the stars for a couple of hours, wondering how I could have ended up serving with such a stupid officer. I went back to the hooch where everyone was asleep, lay down on my cot, and forgot about it.

Lieutenant Big had come to Vietnam too senior as a first lieutenant to get leadership of a rifle platoon and too junior to get a rifle company to command. This posed a serious dilemma for his career promotion prospects. His tour was coming to an end, and he understood he needed time as a leader in the field to get an efficiency report that would keep him in the competition when he was evaluated against his peers. This peer ranking is a constant source of pressure in the career military. Any deviation from the most promising path can mean you fall behind your classmates in the promotion parade toward getting a general's star. And once you fall behind. you can never catch up. Lieutenant Big had earlier received an important career assignment out of West Point, namely service as a rifle platoon leader with the 82nd Airborne Division.

However, that was in the States. He didn't have a combat leadership record yet.

Somehow, Lieutenant Big made his case concerning the promotion risk he was running to our battalion commander, who understood the career implications of the problem. Lieutenant Big's career would suffer if he was transferred to another staff job without a very positive mention of combat leadership in his Officer Efficiency Report.

His answer was to manufacture a field operation, a special operation for Alpha Company alone. The company would be divided into two units of two platoons each, one unit led by the company commander, Captain Neilsen, an excellent soldier, and the other unit led by Lieutenant Big. Unfortunately, my platoon was assigned to Lieutenant Big's unit.

Both units carried out an airmobile assault to land in positions several kilometers apart along a narrow dirt road running through the edge of the Mekong Delta. Our captain's unit would serve as a blocking force, and Lieutenant Big's unit was to organize after the choppers dropped us off and sweep along the road toward the captain's position, supposedly driving any VC forces in the area toward the blocking force. This was a standard operational format when we had intelligence of the presence of enemy forces in an area. It would look good when drawn with arrows on the plastic overlay of the battalion and brigade operations maps. It would be presented to division command as another aggressive tactical move by the battalion. However, in this operation, there were no known enemy forces in the area. Otherwise, I doubt that the senior officers would have trusted Lieutenant Big in the field.

It was the end of the rainy season. The rice fields were flooded; the only way to go was to make our way along the road. No real tactical formation was possible. The dirt road was twenty feet wide, and the troops automatically strung out in two columns along the edges, each putting a meter or two between himself and the man ahead of him. Up front, Lieutenant Big and his RTO walked just behind a squad leading the point of the column. My platoon brought up the rear.

It was an extraordinarily quiet and peaceful walk. Under blue skies, the countryside setting was pristine. Green rice paddies stretched in every direction, bisected by small dikes separating different fields. Off in the distance, several hundred meters away on either side of the road, there were lines of palms and occasional clusters of other trees. Not a human being, hut, water buffalo, or machine was in sight. Herons strutted, heads bobbing down occasionally, through the water of the rice paddies. The only noise was the occasional chirping of birds. Of course, we were surely being observed. The file moved along fairly smoothly, which I took as a sign that Lieutenant Big wanted to show his efficiency and close in on the other unit, the blocking group, in good time. Since we presented a nice target, in the middle of the rice fields with little cover, I was happy that we kept moving. But after a couple of hours, we came to an obstacle.

Running directly in front of us, over five feet above the level of the road, we found the wall of a major dike. The delta was crisscrossed with a tremendous dike system that channeled the waters of the Mekong as far as possible into the countryside so more lands could be flooded for rice farming. At the end of the rainy season, this flow reversed and ran back into the rivers. The front elements of our unit, led by Lieutenant Big, climbed up the mud wall and down the other side to find the waters rushing through the canal formed by the dike walls. The word came back to us that the canal, some twenty feet in width, was full of water from the recent rains and the current was strong. We were facing a significant challenge in our countryside walk designed to improve the lieutenant's efficiency report.

My platoon and I were stopped on the road as Lieutenant Big organized the water crossing. I couldn't see the canal or the men working there: the dike wall blocked our vision. We could hear some talking on the other side and an occasional shouted order from Lieutenant Big, but as we waited to cross over, our attention was focused on the tree lines on either side of the road, looking for signs of enemy activity.

The silence was suddenly broken by loud, incoherent yells that then turned to screams. The noise moved rapidly away down the course of the canal. After a minute or two, which seemed like hours, the screaming stopped, and all went quiet. Those of us waiting yelled up front, asking what the hell was going on. The word came back that the dugout canoe they were using to ferry two troops across at a time had turned over. They had been swept away and dragged under by the current. They were gone.

We were all in shock. How the hell could this happen? We were neither under fire nor under any time pressure at all, so far as I knew. How could the water crossing be so messed up that we had lost two soldiers?

My platoon and I waited for our turn to be called to climb the wall of the dike, and then descend to cross the canal. Lieutenant Big was now on the other side, so I took a second to ask one of the troopers handling the crossing ropes what had happened. He told me that Lieutenant Big had ordered the soldiers to keep their web gear on, with the ammo pouches, hand grenades, and other items strapped to it, so they would be "combat-ready," as he put it, when they reached the other side. Also, although there was a guide rope for the dugout strung across the canal, no safety rope had been provided downstream for soldiers to catch onto in case they fell into the water. Now that the danger had been highlighted with the loss of the two men, soldiers were taking off their web gear and holding it in one hand as they sat in the dugout making the short crossing. There was now a safety rope strung across the canal thirty feet below the crossing point.

Lieutenant Big's deluded idea of being combat-ready, though there was no enemy in sight and the ability of the men to react to enemy fire wouldn't have been impeded if they had their gear in hand, had just killed two men.

My platoon safely made the crossing, and the unit, under Lieutenant Big's direction, continued its "combat sweep" down the road. It was an extremely quiet group of men. We were all in shock. The stupidity and suddenness of the deaths had shaken us. There was nothing to say. Lieutenant Big had, of course, radioed in to the blocking force and the company commander his report of the crossing and the loss of the two men. I believe that was the reason it was decided to bring our day's walk to an end. We came to an area with a dry, elevated field suitable for a helicopter pickup zone. Our unit was ordered to stop there and wait to be extracted by the choppers. Lieutenant Big hustled to the site, arranging the troops in six-man groupings to match up with each chopper as it landed, but it turned out he had one more tragicomic performance up his sleeve.

It is normal practice for troops on the ground guiding in choppers to throw a smoke grenade—we call it "popping smoke"—at one end of the landing zone. This smoke and its color (purple, red, yellow, and so on) identified the landing zone for the chopper pilots and also gave them the wind direction, as they would sweep in to touch down for the troops to jump aboard. As we looked on, I was standing within earshot of Lieutenant Big's RTO as his officer prepared the landing zone for the choppers by popping smoke. But for some reason, he threw not just one smoke grenade at the head point of the landing zone, but then raced around the grid throwing more down on each side and at the other end.

The landing zone was now more like the Twilight Zone, with multi-colored smoke swirling in all directions. The cursing over the radio from the flight leader of the chopper group was magnificent in its originality and venom. There was no way he was bringing his flight in to land in the swirling, smoky haze Lieutenant Big had presented. He led a go-around with the choppers as he waited for the haze to clear, meanwhile asking Lieutenant Big what the hell he thought he was doing.

Lieutenant Big answered, "I was marking all sides of the zone for you."

The answer was so incredible in its stupidity that the flight leader was silenced. He said nothing for a few seconds and then, as the smoke and haze cleared, called down, "We're coming in now."

Of course, we could be sure he relayed the whole incident later to our battalion commander in the most vivid of terms. Nothing would compensate for the loss of our two men, but as I sat in the chopper taking me back to base camp, I was comforted by the belief that Lieutenant Big's career was surely pretty much over. I wasn't certain what he would end up doing, but if there was a God in Heaven, he would never be given the chance to lead men in the field again.

About three days later, we got word that the bodies of our two missing men had been recovered, thanks to a South Vietnamese army unit patrolling the river. The bodies had become entangled in the lower branches of the mangrove trees growing along the river's banks. I had no idea how the tremendously powerful and untrustworthy public relations program of the U.S. Army would describe their deaths to the families, but they would be listed as non-combat casualties, which can amount to as much as one-sixth of the men lost in any of our military adventures. Almost without exception, some form of leadership incompetence leads to these types of deaths. That is a fact the U.S. military public relations machine finds inconvenient to share with the public. For me, it started a personal campaign to ensure that neither I nor the men I led would die of stupidity, be it ours or that of others.

I have never forgotten those sounds—first surprised shouts, then panic-stricken yelling, and then terrified screaming for help as those young men were swept down the canal and underwater, dragged down by their saturated web gear and then bobbing up to scream again once or twice, understanding they were doomed, possibly desperately clutching at the slick mud walls of the canal—mud that had been dredged up by hand from stinking primeval muck laid down on the river delta over a 10,000-year span. Then the even greater shock, the absence of noise, the terrible, terrible silence as they disappeared under the rushing dark brown water for good. They deserved so much better of their leaders, but somehow I doubt the army let their families know that as they joined the other 135 non-combat deaths recorded by the military in Vietnam that October.

Chapter Four

CAMPING—1998-2002

During the latter part of my first year at Mercy, Khun Jai and the Soi 40 girls would provide me with a major opportunity to be of use.

The Soi 40 warehouse and girls' home had become my usual stopping point on the way to or from the Mercy Centre. At Soi 40 I would check in, talk with Tim Hague, possibly spend a minute or two with Fr. Joe if he was in his office, and often, in the afternoon around 3 p.m. or so, relax and talk with the house mom, Jai, as the kids came home from school.

After my experience with the AIDS hospice, it was clear to me that I didn't have the knowledge or emotional strength to continue there. Some weeks afterward, I was talking with Jai and asked her to let me know if there was anything I could do for her and the Soi 40 girls that would be helpful. If I could do it, I would. She put me off for a day or so and then came back to me. She was excited and got straight to the point.

"Khun Tom. The girls want to go camping!" She said the kids were really excited about the possibility of taking the upcoming October school semester break, "pit term" as the Thai say, to leave the city and go camping.

Okay, camping was one of the things I did. I had gone through the army's Jungle Expert School prior to my assignment to Vietnam years before. I had taken up the sport of orienteering, finding my way running through the woods with a compass, in the years after my military service continuing right up the present day. Also, I had taken my son and daughter camping along the Appalachian trail as they were growing up and had tried to pass on some orienteering knowledge. In addition, as part of my off time since arriving in Thailand, my wife and I had already sought out and hiked in a number of national parks. Thailand holds some of the greatest patches of jungle territory in Southeast Asia. Elephants, tigers, deer, Siamese crocodiles, hornbill birds, and other wildlife were there to be found.

However, I had a concern. I didn't think the girls were looking for or up to a campout matching my experience. These were city girls, aged six to fifteen. What was Jai's idea of camping for them? How far would we travel? How long would we be gone? What level of roughing it would be appropriate? What type of support would Mercy be able to provide?

So Jai and I talked and planned. The destination was to be Khao Yai, a national park just over two and a half hours' drive north of Bangkok. It was the nearest park to Bangkok but also a worthwhile one to me, as it was a mountain park covered with jungle, with some attractive waterfalls but decent roads getting in and good campsites near the park rangers' grounds. We would be taking over twenty kids and five staff, including Jai, in addition to myself.

Jai threw me a bit of a curve, though, when she suggested I check to see if any of the park cabins might be available for the girls to stay in. That stumped me for a bit. When I went camping, I didn't consider park cabins. My experience had been to sleep on the ground under a small tent.

However, in this case, I had some good luck. My opportunity to come to Mercy was due to the economic crash. The company I was with had closed its Bangkok office. I called my former secretary and asked for advice on how to contact the park authorities to inquire about some cabins. It turned out that she was dating a pilot in the Thai Air Force stationed at the Korat air base, about fifty minutes' drive north of the park. She spoke with him and learned that the air force had some cabins at Khao Yai they used as a rest area for air force families. He was able to secure four large ones in the park for the Mercy kids. The girls would be doubling and tripling up and many sleeping on the floor, but that would be fine.

The question of how Mercy might help with travel issues was resolved quickly. There would be no help. If the foreigner (me) wanted to take the kids camping, it was up to the foreigner to solve the problems. Another Mercy learning point for me.

Okay, we would need two vans. I made arrangements to rent the vans. I could drive one, but who would drive the second van? Jai went to lobby the admin people a bit and was able to have two of the driving staff, Suchin and Prachoop, assigned to help with the trip and drive the second van. Uncle Suchin was in his mid-forties, was always cheerful, and would turn out to be one of the stars of the trip.

Our trip that day was to be from one jungle to another. Bangkok is a dense jungle of a city, an urban jungle, as they say. At that time, greater Bangkok had a population of over seven million people. Except for the financial and commercial areas, these people were crowded into cheap, low-rise, low-rent apartment blocks which abounded throughout the city. Overhead expressways and two rail lines ran through the middle of town. The streets were always crowded with cars, motorbikes, and pedestrians. It took just a few minutes to go from the port area to connect to an overhead expressway, rising above many of the Klong Toey slum houses underneath. Jai rode up front with me while I drove to help as a guide, but I knew the general route from my previous hiking expeditions.

The ride up to Khao Yai was a school kid's adventure. I had forgotten how kids, especially girls, could talk up a storm and maintain their excitement level for hours. Once out of the city, they were impressed by the unfamiliar openness of the countryside and the swaying fields of rice we rode past, which were ready for harvest. It was a bit chaotic, but fun chaos. At Jai's direction, we stopped at a convenience store on the way up and brought some ice cream and snacks for the kids.

There are well-paved roads running up to and through the Khao Yai park, unlike other parks in Thailand, for a reason related to the war in Vietnam years ago. The name Khao Yai means *big mountain*. The top peak is only 4,000 feet high, but it towers over the city and the sprawling province of Bangkok below at sea level. The Khao Yai Park was founded in 1962, and shortly thereafter, the U.S. military installed an up-to-date air control facility at the top of Khao Rom, Khao Yai's highest mountain. The radar station was intended to provide directions to U.S. military aircraft flying in and out of Don Muang, Bangkok's airport dating from prior to World War II. To facilitate military traffic to the radar station, a two-lane asphalt road had been built with entryways from the south and north of the park. At the time of our visit with the Mercy kids, I had not found another national park with such high-quality road access.

The park adventure started when we reached the park ranger's entrance control station about ten minutes off the public highway. There is a fee for entering the national parks in Thailand, and Jai was determined that the park rangers would give special treatment to the kids. Plus, we didn't have park entry fees in our budget. There was an excited conversation with the ranger at the gate, especially on Jai's part as she excels at excited conversations. I understood part of the conversation was about me as the foreigner present in the parade.

Jai finally turned to me with an apology. "Khun Tom, they agree to only charge a small fee for each vehicle, and no fee for the kids. I'm sorry, they want a higher park entrance fee for you."

That is the normal practice in Thailand. The park entry fee for Thai adults might be the equivalent of U.S. $3. The fee for foreigners would be as much as five times that, U.S. $15 a person. Thailand is a tourist country, and they have the mentality, throughout the country, that foreigners could and should pay more. Jai had been arguing with the park staff that I was doing a good deed, "tham boon" as the Thai say, and I shouldn't be charged.

I told Jai not to worry. I would pay and keep the peace. The most important social guideline in Thailand is to not cause embarrassment. Face, as they put it in Asia, is very important. One of the problems we had over the years with volunteers, and that foreigners in general had in Thailand, was an inability to understand the importance of being cool or jai yen (cool heart) as the Thai say. Don't embarrass people. It's not forgiven if you do. The Thai have long memories if they feel someone has embarrassed or not respected them. I paid. We drove in.

The road in was a winding drive, uphill all the way, with dense green jungle extended to the road on either side. Soon the kids started to see monkeys swinging through the trees, which the girls announced in screams to Jai and me. About halfway up the entrance road, we hit the jackpot. We came across a small herd of Asian elephants grazing on the edge of the jungle and visible from the road. I slowed down so the kids could see, but I didn't stop. Asian elephants are smaller than African elephants and much more approachable, but both species can be dangerous when calves are present. I wasn't sure of the situation with the herd we saw, so I slowed a bit but kept moving.

When we arrived at a large clearing in the forest twenty minutes later, we found the four air force cabins. They were simple two-story cinder block cabins of four large rooms, two rooms downstairs and two rooms upstairs. The cabins were a few feet off the side of the road, on top of a small hill that overlooked a cleared basin area of the park. It was not far from the park ranger's buildings, about another five minutes' drive further on, but we were far enough away that we had privacy. There was a big stone circle fire-ring in front of the cabins and small propane gas cookers on the porch area of each cabin.

I thought it was a great site, and the kids did also. They were screaming with delight at the cabins and the view as they piled out of the vans. Jai's two assistants, Kung and Dtim, were immediately being pushed by the girls to assign the cabins. "Where am I sleeping? Who am I sharing my bed with?" Much excitement, screaming, shouting, running around, laughing. Again, chaos of the best kind.

That night, during the meal Jai and her two helpers had prepared for the kids, we had a visitor. It was Tom Cruise from *Top Gun*. Okay, it wasn't Tom Cruise, but as far as the girls were concerned, our visitor was better. Captain Tan, my secretary's air force boyfriend, a fighter pilot who had requisitioned the cabins for us, stopped by to see that we had come in without trouble and were comfortably settled.

Wow. The guy was the stuff of dreams for the girls. He was about five feet ten inches tall, slimly built, and outfitted in his flight suit, wearing his pilot's wings. All those were good things, but the fatal blows were his athletic good looks and tousled after-duty hair combined with a killer Tom Cruise smile. Right then, the trip was a success no matter what else might happen. He said a polite hello to me, but then Jai and the girls took over with a thousand questions and giggles at his smiles and answers. As I sat on the sidelines and enjoyed all this, what interested me was that it wasn't just the kids who were excited. Jai, Kung, and Dtim were also over the moon. The captain was the night's entertainment and did a great job of charming the girls, young and old alike.

As the captain was leaving, he told Jai and me that he had arranged for a driver to come and guide us up to the mountaintop radar site the next morning. The captain casually mentioned that to check the road and the site out, he had driven up very early the day before. As the road twisted uphill, with the sun rising and the jungle shadows stretched over the road, he had made a turn and, just fifty meters ahead, seen a tiger walking slowly across from one side of the road to the other. Exciting. I had heard from a wildlife conservation friend that there were still tigers in the jungle of Khao Yai Park, but it was different to have it confirmed by an eyewitness. He said that there was a chain-link fence around the radar site but that the brush grew up close to it and often the staff could see wild pigs running through the bushes. His opinion was that the tiger he saw was hunting the wild pigs. When Jai shared that story with the girls it seemed we had cornered the world market on big eyes. A great adventure awaited.

I woke about 6 a.m. the next morning, stirred by military memories. I could hear a drill instructor calling out his troops. Someone was directing the girls to fall out into a two-line formation facing him in front of the cabins. I walked to the window and saw one of the drivers, Uncle Suchin, calling the girls out with Jai cheering him on from the kitchen area. Then, after leading them through some stretches, the girls all sleepy, some moaning, some chatting, he led the column off on a morning run. Hut one, hut two, hut, hut. It was an unbelievable sight. I understood as I thought about it. The girls were not in school, they were camping, and a vigorous lifestyle was to be part of camping. The girls seemed to be enjoying the martial experience. It was clear to me that Uncle Suchin wouldn't be pushing them too hard. He was laughing and chatting with the girls as they went. I was impressed. He was a hero. Well done, Uncle Suchin.

The next few days and nights were good but anticlimactic after Tom Cruise's visit. We did a night ride through the open basin area adjacent to our camp, spotlighting for animals, and saw some smaller specimens of raccoon-like critters and spotted some deer but otherwise not much. I had brought along several compasses I had in my camping equipment and gave the girls a rudimentary class in map-reading and the use of a compass. Despite my poor Thai language skills, I think several of them actually understood what I was trying to teach. We made the trip up to the radar site: it was enclosed in clouds that day, which made it even more exciting for the girls. In general, we had a great time. When we returned home to Mercy the girls were exhausted and happy.

For me, the trip had provided some insight on how I could be helpful at Mercy. There was no way I could fill the role of staff like Jai, Uncle Suchin, and the counselors, but possibly I could enable them and provide support for the activities they were undertaking. Over the next few years, we had several more camping visits to national parks and some dancing classes were arranged in Bangkok when the girls asked for that. It was tremendously rewarding seeing how happy these poorest of the poor kids could be when anything special was arranged for them. I became a yes-man as far as possible for the staff. It was to be the best and most emotionally rewarding job I would ever have.

Nong Wit

At times we judge people by the wrong criteria. A friend once captured this for me when he emphasized that the important thing is not what we are in terms of status, race, religion, or sex, but rather who we are. We should be considering the character qualities of the person first. An example for me from Vietnam is Lieutenant Big, the officer that led two of our soldiers to their deaths in a hasty and ill-judged river crossing. The what about him was that he was the officer in charge. We had to respect that position, but it wasn't who he was. The who was the incompetent bully.

At Mercy, I was to encounter a case of someone being judged negatively because people felt that what he—or she—represented was unacceptable. The young boy's name was Wit, but Wit wasn't a boy, at least in terms of personal identity. Currently, the word used is *trans* or *transgender*. In Thailand, the term for those biological males who identify with the female gender is *katoey*. Wit was a very bright and appealing twelve-year-old katoey.

Wit had been brought to Mercy, as had several children over the years, by a phone call from some responsible person in the Patpong red-light district. Wit was being used as an outside attraction to bring customers into a bar. When our staff brought Wit to Mercy, Wit was in work attire: feminine clothes and make-up. The boys at Mercy are not always a gentle group, and several were on Wit right away, teasing Wit for not being a real boy. They asked Wit if Wit played football (soccer in the U.S.). Wit told them no. Wit had no interest. The boys all laughed, including the counselors; football was everything to our boys and indeed to our male staff. If Wit couldn't play football, what kind of boy was he? Of course, "he" wasn't a boy. Wit's identity was certain in Wit's own mind. He—she—was female.

One of the senior counselors came to me a couple of days later and told me the story, laughing about it. Not a mean laugh, just amazed. He also couldn't conceive of a "boy" who didn't want to play football.

Mercy has a special school for kids who have fallen out of, or never been in, the government school system. It is named the Janusz Korczak school, after a famed Polish educator and promoter of children's rights who died in a Nazi death camp during World War II. The goal of the school, with a Thai government license, is to bring the students up to the level of education required for their age group. Then they will transfer to a government school. Wit had been assigned to that school, on the third floor of the office building. I worked on the second floor, and the counselor suggested I go up to see Wit.

I went up and talked to the teacher who was overseeing a group of fifteen kids ranging in age from ten to sixteen. She was much less concerned with Wit's gender identity than the male counselors. In fact, she was an enthusiastic supporter of Wit. Wit had impressed her, in just a few days, as being one of the brightest students she had ever worked with. Wit was learning quickly and had an open, friendly personality. I went to speak with Wit and was impressed also. The youth was special, with a gentle manner and a ready smile. I took a picture of Wit in class and felt I could just see the light of intelligence shining from those eyes. Of course, Wit liked the attention and was not shy of the camera.

Several of the other volunteers at the time, Mary McLean and John Padorr, came by at different times and were also impressed with Wit's personality. Though we didn't use the pronoun Wit would prefer, we would say, "He's a bright kid. He'll go far." But that was not to be, at least within the bounds of Mercy.

A few days later I went up to the Janusz Korczak school to check on the students, as I usually did. As I looked around, I saw that Wit wasn't there. I asked the teacher, and she didn't know where Wit was. Then, I met with Khun Samran and asked him. He told me that Wit had been transferred to a government home for boys. It wasn't a correctional institution, but certainly, it would be much sterner than Mercy. I was dismayed. Putting a kid who was so attractive, and whose identity was female, in with a group of rough-edged teenage boys seemed to me to invite disaster for Wit.

At that time, Tew Bunnag, a Thai writer and great friend of Mercy and mine, was visiting from his home in Spain and spending time each day at Mercy helping out. Tew's family contact with Mercy went back to the mid-Eighties, and he was much more plugged into the whys of Mercy's doings than I was. I went to him, expressed my concerns, and asked him why Wit had been moved.

He said the decision was made because the senior staff learned that

Wit was born in Cambodia, not Thailand. If Wit spent several years in the government home, the government would consider Wit eligible for a Thai identification card when Wit came of age. That was a key requirement if Wit was to be allowed to stay in Thailand. Thus, the decision was made. It would be better for Wit's future if Wit went to the government home. I was really upset because it seemed to me that while Wit's future might be brighter, Wit's now, for at least the next few years, would probably be dark. Tew thought as I did, but also understood that this was Mercy management dealing with the issues as efficiently as they could. As volunteers, we were mostly just bystanders.

I had expressed my concern to Khun Samran and he kindly invited me to ride along as he and another member of the staff were going out to visit the government home the next day. I was relieved. I thought at least our visit would be a show of concern for Wit to the government people administering the home. Bangkok had grown to a city of over 9 million by then. It was somewhat like Los Angeles in that there was the city proper and then the greater metropolitan area. In Bangkok, that area was spread into a population of 13 million. It took over an hour for the van to wend its way through the city to its outskirts, where the government home for boys was.

Though Khun Samran had called ahead and we were expected, when we arrived, the guards had not been told we were coming. They told us to wait and phoned inside to the administration office. After the call, the guard turned back to us and said that unfortunately, the boy we had come to visit (Wit) was not available due to scheduled activities within the home. We had no choice but to leave and try to reschedule.

The long ride back to Mercy was silent. We were all unhappy and I think Khun Samran was embarrassed at the way the government staff had treated us. It wasn't his fault, and it was an important lesson to me. Government officials can be the same around the world. They had established that they were important and we were not. It was their turf and Wit was now their charge. I came to appreciate the difficult nature of Khun Samran's work even more. He also had the duty to visit the jail holding teenagers being held for various, mostly minor, offenses. This trip had shown me that it was a hard duty, but he was a hero. He would not be turned away, and over the years succeeded in bringing many of the boys into Mercy. He would keep trying to check on Wit. I had to accept that.

I should be clear that my concern was not about Wit's life's evolution. It was concern about how Wit would be able to cope as a transgender person in an intimate setting in a school full of rowdy teenage boys. Hopefully, there were other katoeys Wit could ally with. As an adult, I thought Wit would be fine. Thailand, I believe, is unique in the world in the visible participation in society of large numbers of transgender people. They participate in the professional world, albeit with some discrimination, but they are fully there. Thailand has annual transgender beauty contests for Miss Tiffany Universe, modeled on the straight Miss Universe contest, with the full swimsuit and gown competition. Several years back the *Bangkok Post,* in a beautifully naughty move, waited until after the two queens, straight and transgender, were picked and then ran side by side photos of them in the Post asking their readers to vote on which queen was the most beautiful. To the outrage of women throughout the country, the transgender beauty was overwhelmingly voted the most beautiful.

When I think of Wit now, I see her as a woman, as a beautiful woman, approximately 25 years old. I hope she is doing well in life and is in a good position to care for herself.

Sai the Teddy Bear Girl. Credit Graeme Bristol

Soi 40 warehouse/girls home. Credit Graeme Bristol

Soi 40 camping girls. Credit Tom Crowley

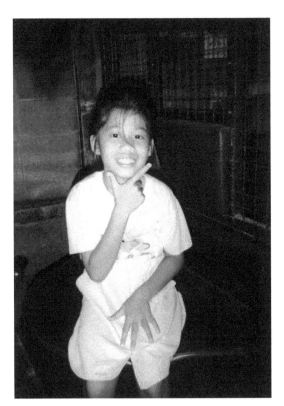

Follow Me Home Girl,
Em. Credit Tom Crowley

The Woodshop boys, Mike Simms at left, Som second from right.
Credit Mike Simms

Nong Wit at school. Credit Tom Crowley

Chapter Five

THE TSUNAMI—
WHAT SHOULD WE DO?—
2004

It was the day after Christmas, 2004. What the Brits call Boxing Day. The tsunami started due to an earthquake, just off the west coast of the Indonesian island of Sumatra, and the city of Banda Aceh, about 7:50 a.m. The tremendous underwater pulse of energy created gigantic waves as the energy surged through the ocean and reached beaches throughout the Andaman Seacoast. The surge and accompanying waves reached Thailand's western shores, villages, and beach resorts about 9:15 a.m. on a sleepy Sunday morning. I imagine most tourists, of which there were many in December, were lazing about after the celebrations of the previous night. No one was prepared or had any idea of what was descending on them.

That is not completely true, however, if you include the animal population. There were many tales afterward from villagers who spoke of their animals, especially the domesticated elephants, which turned and started running for higher ground inland several minutes before the first wave hit. Some eons old preternatural alarm had been sounded, and they responded. Unfortunately, the people, for the most part, just stood and looked and wondered.

There were three giant waves that washed hundreds of meters inland over and through seaside resorts and dwellings, and over the coastal highway. A government patrol boat was even washed over a quarter of a mile inland and left marooned on a hillside just past the highway.

But before the first wave hit, the tsunami pulled the seawater, which had been gently lapping against the beaches, several hundred meters back out to the sea. The rising wave was building up offshore and drawing the beachside water back out along the ocean bottom. For a short period, ten minutes or so, people near the beach rushed out to the flats that had been cleared, picking up fish left on the ground, looking in amazement at this unusual tidal effect. Then, cruelly, leaving them no chance to run to safety, the first mammoth wave roared in. The screaming of the people, many of them children, was silenced by the crushing roar of the watery avalanche, nearly forty feet high, as it descended on the coast.

Tourists and natives alike, walking or resting near the beach, were caught up in the violent, washing machine cycle of the wave. Many, thousands, were never to be found again. Fishing villages were wiped out completely, the bamboo and wooden huts exploding with the force of the water. Sturdier beach houses, small hotels, and commercial properties along the beach road withstood the waves but were completely inundated by the force of the rushing water. Cars were carried away from the ocean road in Phuket up side streets. The first and second floors of beach hotels went underwater. Sleeping occupants were trapped in their rooms and drowned.

The death toll throughout the Andaman Sea area was over 200,000. The official death toll later given for Thailand was about 9,000, though it was said that about 2,000 undocumented workers, mostly from Burma, had died also. Of the official list, most were tourists, and thousands were Swedish: Thailand's beaches were a favorite winter location for the Swedes.

It wasn't until the late afternoon that day that I tuned on the TV news and saw the first images of the destruction that had struck southern Thailand. It was a numbing experience. It was the cool, beautiful season, but there was now a shadow over Thailand. I didn't sleep well, and the next morning I went into Mercy early. I didn't have a plan, but I was feeling the need to do something normal. I had no idea what was going on in the aftermath of the tsunami. About an hour later, Fr. Joe called me, mentioned the tsunami, and asked me to come over to his residence. I thought possibly he was calling a staff meeting, but when I got there, I was the only one. He had the TV on with the news showing, over and over, the impact of the waves, the screams and cries and the destruction that had taken place just the day before. After a while, neither of us could take it anymore and

Joe turned it off. We sat silent and then Joe turned and looked at me and asked, "What do we do?"

Besides the enormity of the question, I knew him well enough by this time to know he wasn't looking for an answer from me. He got up and started walking in circles in his living room. I sat back. As he walked, he talked, mostly to himself, occasionally glancing at me but not looking for any answer from me except possibly a nod to go on.

We spent a couple of hours in that mode. Joe subsequently said, "What do we do? We work with the poor. We help rebuild homes after fires, we provide food and construction aid after slum fires and flooding. We unite families that have been torn apart. We have skills and knowledge that can be used."

At one point I interjected, just pointing out that Mercy's skills and knowledge were pertinent in the Klong Toey district of Bangkok, in the Jet Sip Rai slum, but Mercy was unknown in the area hit by the tsunami. The disaster area was a long, long way from Bangkok. He nodded, took that in, but kept walking, now talking about the type of help fishing villages and those near the shores would need. Homes would have to be built, schools repaired, school materials restored, water jars provided. (Water jars would be a critical need. Virtually all of these fishing village homes got their drinking water from catching and storing the annual eight months of rain in large water jars to see them through the four months of no rain.)

Finally, he stopped and said, "We'll call a meeting and discuss this with Sr. Maria and the staff. After lunch. Come back then." I got up to leave and he said thanks.

I asked "What for? You were doing the talking."

He said, "No, thanks for being here. Thanks for listening."

Good enough. I understood my role and was happy to fulfill it.

It was a somber staff group that gathered that afternoon. Everyone had seen video of the mountains of water, of people screaming and dying. They all understood that Mercy could help in the emergency response in some way. As Joe said to me in our morning meeting, that was what Mercy did. The questions were what and who and how. The presence of Sr. Maria was important. Joe could direct the staff to go along with ideas on aiding the reconstruction in the south, and they would go along, even if they had reservations about the difficulty of working on a new and distant scene. However, if Mercy as a whole was to commit, Sr. Maria's blessing was important. Much of her role at Mercy was to keep Fr. Joe grounded. There would be reasonable concerns about how an organization, already at the limits of its capabilities in Klong Toey, could extend itself in what would be a very costly operation several hundred miles away.

We assembled in the living/dining room area of Joe's house on the Mercy grounds after lunch. We had several levels of Mercy's leadership from differing programs, over twenty people in all. I was sitting on the side, trying to stay out of the way. Several of the staff glanced at me as they came in, possibly wondering what my role might be in a general management meeting. I was also wondering. I was seldom invited to such meetings. In my mind, I had no role to play in the discussion. I was to find out Fr. Joe had a different plan.

Joe started the discussion walking in the center of the small circle the staff had left open when they took their seats, most sitting on the floor. They had seen the TV broadcasts of the death and destruction the tsunami had wreaked in the coastal areas of the South. There was a questioning sense in the air. Why were we meeting? What did this disaster, so far away, have to do with us and Mercy?

As Joe walked, he repeated his thoughts and the points he had made in his earlier walkabout in front of me. This time, he would pause at one point or another to reaffirm with a staff manager in a certain area that we had an area of expertise that could be of use in the South. He spoke to Khun Virat, nicknamed Choi, who oversaw much of the planning and reconstruction after a slum fire in an area near Mercy, and Khun Phakaporn, nicknamed Prong, a manager in Mercy's community outreach program. "Isn't that something that we know how to do?" Of course, the manager would reply yes. Of course, we could do that. However, in the eyes of the team, you could still see the question, "What exactly has that to do with us and Mercy?"

After an hour of thinking out loud, probing the staff with questions on Mercy's capabilities, and expounding on the needs of the families in the South, Joe finally delivered his decision. "Mercy has the skills that are needed. We can't look away. We must go south. We must get involved and send a team to the areas where help is needed the most and help the reconstruction process."

It was a significant moment. Not that any of the staff objected to his description of Mercy's capabilities and the needs of the tsunami survivors, but we were a relatively small, 300-employee, slum-based community aid program. Someone asked about the programs Mercy was doing at home. How would we continue those programs? Joe was clear. "We will do both." Staff members were glancing at each other. How to do both?

No one had asked where the financial resources were coming from to undertake what would be a very costly effort. It wasn't common knowledge among the staff, but Mercy had operated in the red that year. After the others had spoken, pausing to let the room become quiet, Sr. Maria spoke. "Where will we get the money to do this?"

No one moved. She wasn't challenging Joe, she was just, in her clear, firm way, presenting reality.

I believe it's possible Joe had had this moment in mind since our morning session. He delivered his surprise verdict with a flourish that amazed the staff and floored me.

He turned, somewhat dramatically, and pointed toward me. "Money isn't a problem. Tom will get us all we need."

All eyes turned to me. Could this be? The staff knew I was involved in several areas assisting Mercy programs and was present with Joe at differing times, but this was new to them. I was speechless. Possibly I should have seen it coming, but I hadn't.

Sr. Maria, who hadn't paid me much attention over the years, fixed her laser gaze on me. Maybe my surprise showed, but of course, I had to go along with Joe's play even if I felt he had set me up. I looked Sr. Maria straight in the eye and nodded as confidently as I could muster without words. Yes. I would do my part. I would help get the money.

The decision had been made. Mercy would work in the tsunami reconstruction effort. Joe then exhorted the staff, talking about the need to organize in differing areas and get moving quickly. He wanted the advance team on its way to the South the next morning. He dismissed the general meeting and made plans for a meeting with the advance team. As the staff departed, several glanced at me with a bit of wonder that I would be or could be getting the needed money for Mercy. Sr. Maria gave me a grave look as she was leaving. It was clear to me that she accepted what Fr. Joe had said but was not yet believing. She would be waiting to see what funds could be produced.

I think it necessary to include a word here on the shared beliefs of Sr. Maria and Fr. Joe, and their commitment to the poor. In his first year (1971) at the slaughterhouse parish, Fr. Joe received visits over two days from Mother Teresa, the Albanian nun working in the slums of

Calcutta, who was visiting Bangkok. Joe told me she was known but not famous at that time. His memory of her was that "She commanded any room she was in. There was an aura about her." I imagine the Bishop of Bangkok was asked to provide Mother Teresa an example of the work the church was doing with the poor, and the nearest (and probably the best) example was the slaughterhouse parish he had just inherited. At that time, Sr. Maria had already been living and working in the slum for four years. Fr. Joe introduced her to Mother Teresa. Since Sr. Maria didn't speak English, it was mostly just an exchange of good wishes, but Sr. Maria told him, "Take good care of her, Fr. Joe."

Fr. Joe told me several times over the years of Mother Teresa's visit and repeated what she had said to him at the conclusion of the day. It was very simple. She said, "Serve the poor, Fr. Joe. Serve the poor." He and Sr. Maria never forgot that.

Of course, it made a great impression on the young priest. It was to be his course in life in any case, but her comments gave it added weight. Fr. Joe and Sr. Maria differed in background and some thoughts on procedures at Mercy; however, they both shared an ironclad belief and commitment to what was to be their lives' work. That was to serve the poor. Sr. Maria just added a bit of practicality to Joe's constant desire to rush to the latest challenge, whether it be addressing the needs of the HIV/AIDS community or hurrying to attend to any slum fire and the homes and lives that needed to be rebuilt, or now to tsunami relief in the south of Thailand.

There were times that I thought Joe was lost without an emergency. The tsunami provided one, and both Fr. Joe and Sr. Maria were committed. The question was how to do it and not damage the work Mercy was doing in Klong Toey. Fr. Joe just brushed the issue aside; Sr. Maria would not do so. Obtaining the extra financing and other help required to stretch Mercy's abilities was critical.

I didn't know if Fr. Joe's including me was planned or just a spur-of-the-moment thought, but I was a bit angry with him as the meeting ended and told him, "Joe, I'm not sure how we're going to get any new money." He just said he was sure we would find a way. Actually, it always seemed to me that Joe just ignored the financial side of things. He wasn't going to be limited by money. That was someone else's problem. Okay. Thanks. Time to get to work.

However, Joe had grounds for throwing some of the fundraising ball to me. This was not a new function for me. In 1999, my wife and I had organized and paid with our own funds for the legal work to organize the U.S. fundraising arm for Mercy, Mercy Centre USA. Also, over 2004, I had inherited a proposal the staff had started, requesting funding from a major Catholic charity, Caritas Austria. The problem was that the Caritas forms were complex and used English business terms (*benchmarks, metrics,* and others) that the person completing the forms needed to understand. In addition, they required the submittal of relevant spreadsheets. Caritas Austria considered the original application from two senior staff to be lacking, and Mercy had been in danger of losing the offered funding. I was asked to take over the application, redo it with the help of the accounting department, and get it to Caritas. Happily, one strength of Mercy turned out to be the accounting department in the person of Kuhn Punnipa (Nong) and her staff. She provided all the backup I needed. We got a 50,000-euro donation and we had been given a follow-up application to work through in the coming year.

One of the lessons I had learned in Vietnam was the importance of teamwork, of everyone in the unit knowing their role and doing their job. Thus, six years after coming to Mercy as a businessman looking to be helpful in any role, I had found my most useful role on the Mercy team was finance-related work. I didn't mind. I wasn't trapped in the office but was required to go to the streets or work sites to have firsthand knowledge of what was being done and what was needed. Of course, I was only able to do it as I had come to know the staff well. They knew and trusted me with what they considered to be Mercy's financial secrets.

Actually, I deserved little credit. Over the following months, we didn't need to find donors. They found us. The world wanted to give money for tsunami relief. There was, on the part of corporations and aid organizations flush with money, an almost desperate desire to be seen to respond to a tragedy displayed on TV screens around the world. When we were connected, usually through corporate contacts in Bangkok, donors were grateful to find a qualified, street-based, charitable foundation, such as Mercy, who could take their tsunami donations and put the money directly to work.

In the end, many major partners emerged to support the various projects Mercy delivered.

Galong Gets a Real Job

Galong, who has Downs Syndrome, has been a part of our Mercy family for over fifteen years. He originally was brought in as an adult by our street-kids outreach staff in response to a call from the Pratunam district of Bangkok. Galong was working as a doorman at one of the bars trying to entice passersby to come inside. The caller was concerned that Galong was being abused by the bar owners and felt he would be safer and happier at Mercy.

A few years after he found a home with us, we enrolled Galong in our three-year kindergarten at Mercy Centre. He wore a more adult-sized version of the blue shorts and white shirt uniform of the school and he liked that. He loved school—so much so that he graduated from kindergarten twelve consecutive years. For all those years, every lunch hour, he would come to the art shop at Mercy and draw a picture. Yes, one picture. For years, Galong drew the same picture daily. It featured an elephant in a country setting with a mother and father figure alongside and one person riding the elephant. Perhaps it was Galong?

Eventually, Galong got bored with the routine, or maybe he felt he was too grown-up for it. He decided to drop out of the preschool, though even now, he cherishes his friendship with his old teacher and still visits her when he has the time.

In recent years, Galong has been quite busy. He found work at a noodle stand down the street from one of our old shelter houses. The husband and wife who run the noodle stand love Galong and were happy for him to be a part of their lives. Every working day, Khun Suwich, a Mercy House dad and member of our Mercy Centre legal aid team, would take Galong to the noodle shop and bring him home to Mercy at the end of the day on a motorcycle. Galong was front and center in the noodle preparation process and never happier.

Nowadays, Galong is in his mid-fifties and has slowed down quite a bit. He spends his days in the younger boy's home at Mercy. He is drawing his picture once again and taking it easy. Retirement? Mai Gung, the house mom, looks after him.

Credit to: John Padorr, a strong Galong
supporter, MercyCentre

Vietnam—November 1966—
Dead Man Walking

There can come a point in combat, for those whose job it is to go out where you know people will be trying to kill you, when as soon as you get the orders and know that your turn has come again, you start to be paralyzed with fear. It can be after involvement in a few firefights or after a few months of action, but normally it's not too long after your first shootout. This can happen to anyone, and everybody has to fight to accommodate their fear and get on with the job. Some don't, and they become the subject of scorn, possibly sympathetic, but scorn nonetheless. Just another "chicken bastard," someone will say, and they'll be right.

Another aspect of this is the phenomenon I have read about among combat troopers is when, one day, a soldier will wake up with the sure knowledge that today is his day to die. There are accounts of soldiers insisting on giving their best buddies certain mementos they had been carrying, possibly for months, or something brought along from home. There are stories of soldiers writing a last note home and giving it to a buddy, asking him to mail it if the soldier didn't survive the day.

My moment came when I had been in country for about two months. During that time, we had only been in one shootout of any real scale and survived with no casualties. There had been a few smaller brushes with VC groups and some sniper rounds coming our way since then. We were mortared in the field at one point, but my platoon had sustained no serious injuries. No one had been killed in action.

The prior day, we had left the field and gone back to the division base camp, and that brought feelings of relative safety. Except for a few mortar rounds coming in, there was no reason to expect serious enemy activity. Then late in the afternoon, I was told that my platoon had been picked for an ambush patrol the next day. It was normal to send out patrols around the division base camp to ensure the VC couldn't bring in mortar units within a thousand or so meters and shell the camp. An area of some 300 meters had been cleared all around the camp to provide fields of fire in case of an attack. The sides of the Cu Chi camp, on the north and east, were fronted by the Filhol rubber plantation.

These rubber trees were a residue of the French colonial occupation. My patrol would go out from a heavily sandbagged outpost on the edge of the camp perimeter known as Ann-Margaret. It was named after the movie star who had visited the camp and that outpost earlier in the year on a USO tour. The plan was simple: we would walk northeast the 300 meters through the open area until we reached the tree line. We would enter the trees for a further 200 meters, so we could be confident our patrol was not being directly observed by VC watchers. Once deep inside the plantation, we were to make a sharp break to the right heading to a trail cutting through the plantation area directly east of the camp and set up an ambush position before dark.

This last instruction highlights the very unusual nature of this patrol. Normally, we left whatever base we occupied to go on patrol just after the sunset. Operating in the dark kept any enemy observers from knowing just how many soldiers might be coming out and what direction they would take. This idea of going out in full daylight, when Charlie would be watching and counting us, concerned me. I didn't like it, and I knew the troops wouldn't like it.

In the morning, I went over to the battalion operations center to get the patrol orders. I was able to go over the route and plan with the operations officer designated as the battalion S3, a major. I had done this in one form or another many times before and handled my nerves well, but for some reason that day I was sick with apprehension. I was shocked at my fear. I had awoken that day feeling that I was doomed, and I just couldn't shake the sensation. This premonition was strong and grew stronger throughout the day.

Back at my hooch, I called a meeting with the two squad leaders who would be going out with me and briefed them. In addition to myself, my radio telephone operator, and our medic, the total number on the patrol would be twenty men taken from their two squads rather than the full platoon of forty. Trucks would come for us at 2 p.m. and take us to Ann-Margaret, where we would walk out through the wire surrounding the division base camp. We would inspect the troops and their gear, ensure that all was in order, and prepare to leave the outpost at 3 p.m.

My fear continued to grow as we boarded the trucks. When we reached the outpost, I barely had the strength to climb down off the truck. The atmosphere that day matched my mood: it was hot as usual but overcast and the air felt heavy and gloomy. I was wondering if my fear was showing as I inspected the men, their weapons, and their gear before going out. Normally, I would make a joke or two and try to relax the men I was leading. On this day, I was speechless and so scared I wanted to puke but couldn't. After the inspection, I just turned to the squad leader whose men were taking point and told him to lead us out, indicating the compass direction to follow. My fear grew as we zigzagged our way through the wire. I felt as if I was going to my death, and I didn't want to die.

The physical act of walking didn't calm me down, but it did allow me to think a bit. In that 300-meter walk to the tree line, my mind was swirling, thinking about how I didn't want to disgrace my family or let my men down, and at the same time thinking about how much I didn't want to die. I was thinking about the life I had yet to live. Each pace seemed like a step closer to death. In my mind, I was a dead man walking. The fact that my men and squad leaders were all experienced meant that there was no talking as we made our way out. Perhaps many were having the same thoughts I was having. Or perhaps, knowing what a good target we made as we emerged into the open, they were just super-focused on the area around us. The silence helped me greatly as I wrestled with my fear.

Somehow, during those 300 meters, I found resolution. It came to me that there were things worse than death and that I had to cling to that thought. I reached a form of acceptance. I was dead. I was dead and should accept it and get on with my job.

If not today, then on another patrol or air assault in the future, I was going to die, and that had to be okay. When I accepted that I was dead, I was able to come to terms with the needs of the day. Not that I lost my desire to live, and as we started to enter the tree line, I was actually more intensely focused on our surroundings than before. Somehow, I knew that I could do my job as I had accepted the worst that could happen. I don't know in detail how other men handle that fear of death or a premonition as strong as I had experienced, but I am sure that over thousands of years, many legions of warriors have walked down the same emotional path that I had just traveled and come to the same conclusion. Accept death and get on with the job. In retrospect, I don't see how it could be done otherwise, and that was my route.

Once we had passed the tree line and had traveled a further two hundred meters or so, I passed the word up the line to stop and went forward to talk with the point squad leader. As we were getting closer to the ambush area and I had ceased to be so absorbed with myself, I could now sense the tension building in the patrol. I gave the squad leader the new compass direction through the trees of the rubber plantation, and we headed out.

At that time, I had no knowledge of rubber trees or rubber plantations (though I would become very familiar with them over the passing years, living later in Malaysia and Thailand). Actually, a walk through a rubber plantation can be a lovely experience. The trees are not large, generally fourteen to eighteen inches in diameter and twenty or so feet high. They are evenly spaced about ten feet apart and run in straight ranks for hundreds of meters, so you can see between the rows quite a distance ahead and to your left and right as you walk along. The sunlight, weak on this day, provided patches of illumination between the dark spaces in the shade of the foliage, and the overall effect was of a series of connecting and dimly lit tunnels. There was not a sound, no birds singing, nothing. The ground was moist and soft underfoot as the rainy season had recently ended, so the footsteps of the troops as they walked along were muffled. The tension continued to rise while we walked further into the rubber plantation, the men half-crouched now, prepared to hit the ground and start firing at the first sign of Charlie in the neighborhood. I had moved a bit farther up the line, wanting to ensure we were on the right compass heading without yelling or making any noise. I could see the point man about fifteen meters in front, and the squad leader would occasionally look back to me so I could guide him along with my hands—a bit to the right, a bit to the left, or straight on.

Part of being a leader in any setting is having a mastery of the required skills. For some reason, I had always been at the top of my classes when it came to map-and-compass work. This was an extremely important skill for infantry leaders in Vietnam, though I understand these skills have been trumped today by the use of GPS systems. I had no doubt I would get us to the point on the map we had been ordered to reach.

We had been out a little over two hours, and despite my newfound peace with myself, I was beginning to be afraid that we had gotten off course, when the point man finally stopped and turned, waving the squad leader up. After a minute or so, it was the squad leader who turned and waved me up as well. I told my RTO to stay in place and went to the front. We had come to the dirt trail on which we were supposed to set up the ambush and spend the night. The point man went forward and carefully looked up and down the trail, studying it. When he returned, he told us he had found a set of bicycle tracks, fresh and deeply etched into the somewhat muddy trail. The VC used bicycles as mini-trucks, loading them down with heavy 100- or 200-pound rice bags and walking the bikes along. This seemed to have been the case here.

The question was, what to do next? This was the trail we had been sent out to find and the fresh bicycle tracks indicated that the VC were using the trail to transport supplies, so it showed promise. If we set up the ambush here, we would have a good chance to surprise them if they came along during the night or early morning. However, it was still light. The shadows of the trees were growing longer, but it was only a little after 5 p.m., and I estimated we had a good thirty to forty-five minutes before dark. I thought it would be foolish to set the men in ambush positions right there and take a chance on the VC spotting us before nightfall. I told the squad leader we should follow the trail further along toward the small, deserted village shown on our map and see what we found. If we didn't find anything in twenty minutes, we would double back through the plantation and set up the ambush along the trail after dark.

If I had thought the men were alert as we walked through the rubber plantation, the effect of reaching the trail and getting the word about the fresh bicycle tracks took the tension and their response to a whole new level. I could see it in their eyes. Of course, there was fear there, but that, under control, was a good thing. I could see several men setting their M-16s on automatic, just as I did.

We set off, not in single file now, but two abreast on either side of the narrow trail, ready to drop into the bordering brush if necessary. The point man was leading with an older model M-14 in hand as he felt this weapon had more punch, and another soldier with an M-16 was walking across from him. The squad leader came next, then two more soldiers and then myself with my RTO behind me. I might have been a bit further up front than the book would say I should be, but I felt I had to be able to see what came up, as the time for hand-signals and waving troops around would be minimal if we came across any VC.

It was only a five-minute walk until we came to an opening in the trail, and the sight of the first thatched-roof hut. Off to the left of the opening, we saw a stack of sharp stakes that had been prepared for use in punji pits, the camouflaged holes the VC would dig for U.S. soldiers to fall into where they could impale themselves on the sharpened stakes. This was surely Charlie's home. It was originally a farmer's village that the VC had now turned into their camp. As we took several steps toward the hut, we could see what the U.S. military would call "stacked arms" in front of it—five or six rifles leaning up against one another, butts on the ground and barrels pointing upward. We could hear the singsong cadence of Vietnamese voices coming from inside the hut. We had caught Charlie taking his dinner break.

Being with experienced troops is everything in combat. As we entered the small clearing, I had pulled up even with the squad leader and point men. Without my having to say a word, the troops behind us had approached and moved to either side of us, forming a line facing the hut. Now we could see, through the trees behind the first hut, several other huts spread out in the small camp. I registered that there were many more VC around than the five or six men in the hut, but that thought was interrupted by a sudden silence.

The VC inside had stopped talking. They must have heard something. The squad leader had motioned our machine gunner, Spec. 4 Bill Cline, up front to join the line facing the hut, but I had heard nothing.

It didn't matter. In a few seconds, the VC came running out of the hut, reaching for the rifles they had stacked outside the door while they ate. The squad leader barked at the machine gunner to get them, but he didn't have to say a thing. This man had been in Vietnam over eight months and knew what to do. He was Rambo years before that name became known. He held his M-60 machine gun against his hip with the left hand on top of it to keep the barrel from running up as he fired. He calmly and coolly opened fire, sweeping back and forth across the group of VC and gunning them all down. You may say they never had a chance, and any combat soldier will tell you that's a good thing. Never give the enemy a chance. That only puts you and your buddies in danger.

There were a few seconds of silence after the machine gunner stopped firing. I had just started to think of what to do next when the VC answered for me. We started taking fire from further inside the camp. Almost immediately off to my right, a tree seemed to explode about twelve feet above the ground. I found out later the other squad leader, Staff Sergeant Johnson, had spotted a VC lookout in the tree. For whatever reason, Johnson had carried along an anti-tank missile, a

LAW, and fired it at the man. If it had hit the VC, I doubted it would have exploded, but rather it would have gone through him. As it was, it seemed to have hit the tree and exploded, still killing him.

The explosion just lent emphasis to my decision. Going into the camp and taking fire from every direction didn't seem a smart thing to do. I noticed the trail led off to my right, staying outside the camp. I called to the men to move off in that direction, remaining outside and firing into the camp. The point man and another soldier headed down the trail in front of me, and after ten paces or so, we came to a trench we had to jump over. Just before I jumped, I saw a VC, about twenty feet up the trench line, stand up and raise his weapon in my direction. Before I could react, one of my men, or possibly several of my men in file behind me, shot him down. At this point, there was so much shooting going on it was hard to know who was firing at what, but again I was thankful I was with an experienced group of soldiers. They knew what to do when Charlie was present—shoot, shoot, and shoot again, and no time for questions.

We had moved some fifty to sixty feet along the trail and were approaching the other side of the camp. There was a relatively dry rice paddy ahead, with an embankment or small dike running parallel to the village. I thought that would be a good place to put the troops into position to take the VC in the camp under fire.

Moving troops under fire is a difficult thing, especially when you are moving away from it. It's easy for panic to set in. I stopped and stepped off the trail to try to organize the move better, as our movement along the path had turned into a run, and I knew we had to keep fire on the VC. If we all ran to cover with no one firing back, we would be a great target. My RTO stood next to me and I touched each soldier as they went by, telling them to slow down and keep an eye on their backs.

After two or three men had passed, there was a tremendous explosion just off to my right. I was picked up and thrown ten to twelve feet through the air before hitting the ground. I thought I was dead. I remember thinking as I flew through the air, in what seemed to be slow motion, *Now I'm going to meet God.*

Then I hit the ground. I was back to reality, and amazingly enough, I still had my M-16 in my right hand. I stood up and heard a horrible screaming. It was my RTO. He hadn't been blown off his feet, as I had taken most of the blast, but he had taken several pieces of shrapnel in his legs, one of which had nicked his scrotum. He was going into shock, screaming, "They've shot off my balls. They've shot off my balls."

I was in a bit of a shocked state myself, but told him, "Shut the fuck up. We'll get the medic to look at it."

The troops from further back in the file were still coming along the trail. I pushed my RTO onto the trail and told him to move along. I counted several more soldiers, and then one of them told me he was the last man. I backed onto the trail and then out into the clearing toward the dike, firing short bursts back into the camp. I had to change the magazine along the way and just threw the used one in the dirt, not wanting to take the time to carefully stow it back in the ammo pouch. I turned when I was halfway across the field and yelled at my RTO that I needed the radio. He shouted back that it had been hit by shrapnel and wasn't working.

Now I was closing on the dike, conscious that my men were down in position, firing back into the camp, and that we were taking fire from it. I called out that I needed the damn artillery radio if my battalion radio wasn't working. I was moving a bit slower now: I had taken shrapnel all up my right side—leg, arm, and head. I finished another magazine and then one of the squad leaders emerged from behind the dike and helped me into place. Another brought the radio over.

The medic came to me to look at my wounds and I asked him about my RTO. He told me he would be okay. The shrapnel had just nicked his scrotum. He had bled a bit but was still serviceable in the medic's opinion. There were nine other guys with wounds, though apparently none were serious.

While the medic bandaged me up, I was able to get through to the battalion operations center on the radio and let them know our situation, that we had eleven wounded and were up against a possible platoon of VC, maybe twenty or thirty in number, and taking automatic weapons fire. After giving them our position, which was on the other side of the camp from where we initially intended to set up the ambush, they linked me up with artillery and I was able to start calling in artillery fire on the camp area. The battalion CO told me they would be sending a mechanized infantry company out to relieve us, but that it would take several hours or more to arrive as it was now dark.

At one point, the operations officer asked if I wanted a medevac chopper to lift out the wounded. I told him no. Having a chopper land after dark in the open field between the two sides shooting at each other would just pose an unnecessary danger to the chopper crew and those waving it in to carry out the evacuation. Since I had been told I had sustained the worst wounds so far, I had no reservations in making the decision not to have the medevac.

The rest became increasingly hazy to me as, over the next several hours, the blood loss and shock set in. At last, I told the artillery to check fire, and I gave up the radio to one of my squad leaders at about 10:30 p.m., when we saw the armored personnel carriers (APCs) coming into sight. I was loaded into one and passed out. An hour or so later, I came to as they carried me out of the APC into the division hospital surgery room and put me on an operating table. My battalion CO came over and told me he was proud of us, that we had done a great job. I remember telling him that I thought we had screwed up since it was such a crazy shootout. Then I passed out again.

So it hadn't been my day to die after all.

Chapter Six

TSUNAMI RECONSTRUCTION 2005–PRESENT

I t's understandable, but there was a serious flaw in the reports of the tsunami made by the U.N. and other aid agencies. They lost the individuals in their summaries and thus lost the real stories.

Their reports lack the story of the fishing village mom who lost track of her two young boys as the tidal wave swept them under and forward as they ran from the wave. She somehow survived but could not find the boys. They were missing. She was in agony, afraid they were dead, feeling that she was somehow responsible. Five days later she would find it was worse than that. The boy's bodies were found, lying close together in a patch of jungle across the coastal road. Possibly they had been alive and able to cling together for a while, enough to keep them close. The searchers who found the boys told her the boys, injured and broken, had landed together and seemingly survived initially only to die of exposure after some time. The woman fell to her knees and broke down in front of the rescue workers as she learned this.

Her pain is the story of the tsunami, repeated in differing forms over and over and over again. A teenaged, handicapped Thai prince was staying with his family at a resort hotel near the beach. As the wave swept in, those looking after him lost track of him and ran for the second floor of the hotel. For whatever reason, the young prince didn't run. He was trapped and drowned on the first floor, which was submerged in water.

There were over 9,000 people dead, thousands of such stories. Of that total, there were over 1,500 people missing. This would be painful to survivors in any part of the world. In Thailand, as a Buddhist country, the families believe that to release the soul to the next life, the body must be cleansed and the proper rituals observed before cremation. The inability to do so was a special kind of pain.

I accompanied the team on one of their early visits. The physical destruction we saw as we drove along the coastal highway from the Phuket airport was enormous. The fishing villages along the coastal area were destroyed. As we drove, we passed the Thai navy patrol boat that had been thrown over a quarter of a mile inland across the coastal road. It sits there today as a monument to the power of the tsunami. In the fishing town of Ban Nam Khem, up to 1,500 homes were destroyed with under fifty left standing. Over 1,000 people were reported to have died there. In the small harbor, larger fishing boats were thrown on top of each other and up on the shore. The town has erected a large golden Buddha statue with its back to the sea. This memorial has now become a tourist attraction.

The pain of the mom who lost her two children, and that of all the people Choi and Prong and the Mercy team spoke to, provided the context for our efforts at reconstruction. The starting point for all of Mercy's work with the poor was simple. First, get the permission of the people. This was a point that Fr. Joe and Sr. Maria stressed to our staff in all of the projects Mercy entered into in the slums in Bangkok. In undertaking the tsunami reconstruction work, we found so many times that larger aid organizations, both Thai and foreign, didn't have this maxim as part of their work approach. Many organizations would approach shattered villages and tell them, "This is what we are going to do for you." Sometimes it would be on a par with what the villagers felt they needed, sometimes not.

The worst example I remember in this regard was an evangelical group from Oklahoma who had rushed over to Thailand to help after the news of the tsunami reached them. We came across the group about a month into our work, when we were driving along a dirt road to a fishing port town that had sustained serious damage. There were a series of bamboo hut fishing villages along the beach road that had been completely destroyed. We saw a big white tent with a red cross on it and a group of Moken villagers, or sea people, sitting at benches around tables inside the tent. Several white folks were walking around inside and outside the tent as we went by.

On the way back out, a couple of hours later, we saw the same situation. We were driving slowly due to the poor condition of the road and one of the Oklahoma group saw that there were white people inside the car and rushed toward us, waving for us to stop. We did so. He approached about ten feet away and shouted, with an Oklahoma twang, "You folks have anyone who can speak Thai?"

We looked toward him and then to the tent, just shaking our heads. What was going on?

He explained, waving toward the tent, "We're getting ready to read the Bible before lunch and none of these people understand English."

I looked inside the tent and saw a podium set up with one of the Oklahoma staff standing at it holding what I presumed was the good book. Amazing. Apparently, the ground rules were that the villagers had to listen to a reading from the Bible, and possibly acknowledge it in some way, before they would be fed.

We were all dumbfounded and paused for a second, then Fr. Joe told the driver, "Let's get the hell out of here."

We left the ardent and woefully unprepared missionary staring after us. We were not the only ones who witnessed such a scene. A few nights later a similar situation—foreigners, a very large white tent with a red cross on top, and benches holding displaced villagers waiting for lunch following a Bible reading—was displayed on Thai TV. The commentator spoke in a blistering manner about the religious arrogance and ignorance of Thailand demonstrated by these "foreign missionaries." He went on to say that this was not the "help" the people of Thailand wanted or deserved.

As we drove away, Fr. Joe was red-faced and angry at what we had just seen. Mercy's work was to serve the people and respect the people. One form of respect is to know them, as Fr. Joe and Sr. Maria did, through living with the poor all their adult lives. Take the time, make the effort to be one with them, before asking permission to serve them. I believe only street-based groups such as Mercy would instinctively follow this path.

Understanding the above gives a basis for understanding Mercy's approach and success in tsunami relief. First, our advance team had to find out what groups they were talking to in estimating reconstruction needs. The population of the Andaman Sea coast included Thai of

Buddhist and Muslim background, as well as a good number of the
Moken, who have their own dialect with no written form and are
animists whose religion is the worship of the gods of the sea. The Thai
government considers the Moken to be a separate people, not Thai.
The Moken in Thailand are an indigenous nomadic tribe, numbering
between two thousand and four thousand, who have lived on and fished
from the islands of the Andaman Sea for over a thousand years. They
usually don't have Thai ID cards and have not been recognized socially
or politically by the Thai government.

The sea coast population that had suffered losses from the tsunami
included all three groups: Thai Buddhists, Thai Muslims, and the Moken.
The first question the Mercy staff asked each group they approached was
the same, "Can we help you?" The second question was "What do you
need?" The villagers would decide what was necessary to get their lives
back to normal. In each case, we found that the village committee,
usually a group of five or six of the older women, had to meet and
discuss what was to be done. Importantly, to maintain village unity,
they had to decide fairly which families were to receive help first. Any
work that could be done by the villagers, we would expect them to do.
Mercy would provide the tools, Mercy would buy building materials,
and Mercy would bring in craftsmen as necessary for special projects.

As an example of special projects, many Moken had lost the
large dugout canoes with outriggers that they used for fishing and
transportation. Mercy found men who specialized in this work further
south in Thailand and persuaded them to come to the destroyed areas at
Mercy's expense. The village might need twelve canoes but would only
get one or two at a time as they were built by hand over the weeks. The
committees would decide who got the canoes as they arrived. We learned,
as we went along, that the committees would usually arrange that the
new canoes be rotated among the needy families in the beginning, so all
households had some access for fishing.

Another special need was water jars. All the village houses used
very large clay water jars, put on the ground at the corners of the water
drains from the roofs, to catch water during the rainy season to see
them through the dry season. Each home would have three or four
jars. The metal water gutters on the roofs and the waterspouts draining
the rainwater down to the jars had to be purchased and installed after
rebuilding the huts. Again, Mercy had to find and bring in craftsmen

from other areas of Thailand to set up small production centers to make these jars. The village committees would decide who got them first. At the end of the work in the south, Mercy had overseen the production and distribution of over 2,500 water jars.

The Mercy team would not undertake work any other group could do. If the team found another group, the Thai Red Cross for example, had started work with a village, we would just go on to another area where our help was needed. Also, though Mercy helped repair and equip damaged schools in the tsunami area, the schools were the long-term responsibility of the government. As in Bangkok, the local teachers turned out to be our best source to find those in need. In our contacts with the schools, invariably primary schools, the teachers would have information on how the students and their families had fared. Through the teachers, we learned of nearby villages that were in distress. The team would approach these villages and initiate whatever help the village committee would invite Mercy to undertake.

So Mercy started. Choi and Prong were there, working on the ground, talking to the villagers every week. Fr. Joe went down to the south often, possibly every other week for a couple of days at a time. The senior leader for Mercy in the south was Khun Usanee, the head of the AIDS hospice program. She provided a knowledge of Mercy, knowledge of medical issues, and a senior authority to interact with village leaders and Thai government officials.

Sr. Maria also went down several times, mostly in the early stages, seeking to understand first-hand what the challenges were and how our staff was taking them on. It was at this time that I learned of the steel in Sr. Maria's spine when she confronted those who would prey on the poor.

An issue that raised its head several times when addressing the assistance needed for the Moken people to rebuild their beachside villages was that many of those villages were on what would be considered prime beach areas. These pristine beaches would be valuable in any country of the world, but they were especially so in a tourist-driven country such as Thailand. There were Thai developers, usually of Thai-Chinese background, who tried to move their own workers onto these village areas to claim the land and initiate construction of a beachside hotel. Their plan was to get something started so that when someone spoke to the government on behalf of the Moken, the developer could claim the land by right of squatter status and then bribe the ranks of government officials to approve their claims. Since the Moken were virtually non-people in the eyes of the Thai bureaucracy, such a plan might well be viable, no matter how loathsome.

One evening, early on, Sr. Maria visited the beach area of a shattered Moken village. Our staff had gathered a large group of the villagers to discuss how best to proceed to help them and protect their land rights. A developer, targeting prime beach sites along the coast, had found this village was on an attractive beach area. Construction equipment had been brought in by the developer and was sitting nearby, poised for the next day's project work, which was to plow the remains of the village under and prepare the grounds as a hotel project site. Our staff was on the scene, explaining to the tribe that under Thai law, the important thing was for them to stay on the site. Moving away would allow the workers for the developer to move in and lay claim.

Belying the calm tropical ocean side setting—the sun descending over the water, the scattered palm trees along the beach, and a soft ocean breeze—it was a very tense scene. As our staff talked with the villagers, a group of thugs hired by the developer made their appearance. They were wearing guns, visible under their untucked shirts and circling the group, calling out, swearing and threatening, trying to intimidate the very frightened village families into moving away. The Mercy staff told me later that it wasn't just the villagers. They too were frightened.

Sr. Maria, seventy-five years old, wearing her full black nun's habit as she always did, moved to stand in the middle of the circle in which the village families were sitting. She was a figure of moral authority, not one to bow to criminal force. She spoke to the families with a strong and clear declaration of unity.

"Do not move. Do not be afraid. This is your land. We [indicating the Mercy staff] will stay with you. Whatever you do keep your place here. If they try to move you, don't go. This is your village ground. The ground of your ancestors. Even if they bring the bulldozers to move you, remain sitting in place. We will be with you."

Bravo, Sr. Maria, directly facing down the guys with the guns.

And so it was. I wasn't on the scene that night, but the staff told me the story a few days afterward. They couldn't believe Sr. Maria's courage and resolve. The Mercy staff stayed with the villagers, and, in the night hours, the thugs had departed. The next day, our staff and the village heads met with the nearest police station and made their claim against the land-grab attempt by the developer. The police agreed, nothing would be allowed to happen until a judgment was made. One important issue was that the Moken had no legal papers for that beach site or on almost any of the hundreds of beach sites the Moken people lived on in Thailand. Eventually, months later, the legal team brought in to assist the Moken tribe was able to produce a map and a census report, nearly a hundred years old, showing that a Moken tribe had been counted and stated to be living at that site. The battle had been a victory for this tribe.

Many tribes, in other areas of the tsunami disaster, lost the battle and their traditional home sites. The developers were ruthless in their exploitation efforts.

The Mercy tsunami team had been motivated to help the people of the many villages that had been destroyed in the south of Thailand before the episode at the beach with the Moken tribe. Following Sr. Maria's example, they were even more inspired to carry on the very taxing work they had begun. I felt the same way. I had always been proud to be part of the Mercy team. Sr. Maria's courage and moral power were inspirational.

The tsunami reconstruction work was to continue for over a year on most projects and longer on some others. As the Mercy team's work became known, local village leaders would come to them and ask that they visit another site that had received no attention and was in need. The world wanted to help.

At the same time, it seems the world has only so much time for disasters. The tsunami destruction was the disaster of the moment, so we felt the pressure to act quickly. My job was to write the proposals to justify the donations and then, afterward, the reports on the work that had been done. We had received many requests for proposals from charitable groups, corporations, and the aid offices of some nations. They all needed specific examples of how we would use the money they entrusted to Mercy. These same donors wanted detailed reports on how the work was done and the end result. I understood that the reports were wanted in a timely fashion to fit into the following year's annual report. Fair enough. To me, the corporate desire to advertise their community support effort was a normal business practice.

I traveled to the south weekly, visiting the team at various work sites, asking questions, taking notes, taking pictures. The staff asked me why I was so inquisitive. I told them that the people who donated the aid money needed to know the details of what we were doing and how we were spending their money. Their innocent answer was, "Why? Don't they trust us?" I told them the donors trusted us, but the reporting was necessary for their shareholders, whether it was government, corporate, or individuals. The staff, all of a social work background and not attuned to the commercial world, just shook their heads but gave me the information we needed.

The head of Irish Aid, Mr. Brendan Rogers, even visited some rebuilt villages in person to see the effect of the Euro 200,000 Irish Aid contribution. He told the team the Irish people would be proud to see how their money was used. His visit helped the team to understand why I asked so many questions.

Fr. Joe supported all the projects the team worked on in the south, but eventually, he was quite taken with one of the Moken projects, on an island a short distance offshore. I think his motivation was both the challenge of the project and that it fit his goal of working with the "poorest of the poor."

It was a unique project, one Mercy would continue up to today. The introduction for the Mercy team came through a request from an elementary school teacher in one of the villages Mercy aided. She asked that we visit another isolated and destroyed Moken village. The teacher was one of the rare Moken who had been able to learn Thai and gain an education. She knew of a village in need on a small island, Koh Lao, a thirty-to-forty-minute boat ride from the fishing port of Ranong. This was a very difficult reach for agencies offering aid, and thus, the village had received none. Fr. Joe asked the team to go to see what the need was and what could be done.

It was a discouraging picture. The village had fifty families and a population of approximately 370. As you approach Koh Lao, one of the first things you see emerging from the green jungle background of the island is the collection of wooden and bamboo homes built on stilts over the water's edge. The homes were not spread out but rather clustered together in one contiguous mass, each house almost touching the other so that it seemed you could walk from the porch of one house to the next and make your way through the village in that manner. Possibly it's done so that a person doesn't have to get down into the water at high tide to make their way around the village. Whether it's cause or effect, it came to me, as I met with them and learned a bit about the social life of the Moken, that they were indeed a close-knit group.

Another thing that quickly became apparent was that Moken people were not living the glorified pastoral life sometimes conjured up in *National Geographic* photo articles but rather a savage daily fight for survival. The people of the village were malnourished. All of the community had intestinal worms that took several treatments over a period of months to eliminate. Mercy's medical staff supervised the administration of the medicine for eliminating the worms and later told me horrific stories of how the worms, often quite large, a foot or more long, would emerge from virtually any orifice of the body. Some villagers would have several worms come out at the same time.

When our Mercy staff first approached this village, they found a horrendous child death rate from disease and malnourishment. There were as many as five children dying of differing causes each month. In the following year, with Mercy assistance and education, only six child deaths occurred in total. Now the community is, for the most part, healthy. Mercy's main program with the children is education, but you have to protect the children and their health first.

Over the following months, into the second year, the Mercy team completed its tsunami relief and reconstruction work on the coast of the mainland. There was one exception. Fr. Joe made the decision that the people on Koh Lao would not be abandoned. The work to help these isolated villagers would continue.

Mercy established a preschool on the island that began teaching thirty-five children the Thai language. The Mercy staff provided medical counseling to the community and, most importantly, provided a nutritious lunch each day. Two years later, Mercy established a home in the port city of Ranong to house ten of the older Moken children so they could attend primary and junior high school at government schools in the city. Mercy undertook the lobbying effort necessary to get the Thai school system to accept the children

That project has continued until today under the guidance of Khun Prong, one of the original leaders of the tsunami reconstruction effort, who I think should be considered the patron saint of the Moken on Koh Lao. Fr. Joe recently sent me a note with the latest numbers. Mercy now has sixty-five kids in the preschool on the island and is assisting another fifteen kids attending a government primary school established on the other side of the island. There are, at present, fifteen children in the Mercy home in Ranong attending the government high school.

Possibly the most amazing number is that nearly 220 Moken, children and adults, have now received Thai citizenship. While the traditional way of life is passing, there is a basis for hope in the future of the Moken children.

Mercy's response to the tsunami was, in my biased opinion, heroic. The Mercy teams that worked the areas struck by the tsunami during the year and more following December 26, 2004, had labored away from their families, for long periods, under very difficult conditions. In the heat of the dry season, and then the later monsoon rains, they searched out the neediest of villages, and brought aid that saved and enhanced countless lives. Mercy aided the people in over twenty-five villages and schools, helped to build homes, assisted the villagers to dig wells or provided water jars when necessary, provided twenty dugout canoes and fishing nets, provided medical assistance, aided villagers to get government IDs, and assisted negotiation with the provincial government to obtain needed government services.

Early on in my tour in Vietnam, I was lucky to be with a team of soldiers that supported each other in difficult times. Now with Mercy, I had found my position in the team, my support role in finance and fundraising. I was merely a witness to this extraordinary grassroots program but very proud to be that.

The Rail Line Kids, Fai and Khao

One of the routes I took to Mercy in the morning included a brief walk under an expressway bridge. A cargo rail line ran next to the expressway and there were a number of men who had fallen on hard times, virtually all alcoholics, who lived under the bridge to escape the rain showers and strong sun of Bangkok. Every workday, I walked under the bridge to access another road corner at which I could catch a motorbike to ride to Mercy.

One day while on my walk, I noted the presence of the men sleeping off their drunk from the night before, but I did not pay much attention until one morning, I saw two young kids, a girl about twelve and a boy about ten, sitting near the men. They were obviously part of the group. Most probably their father was sleeping there. When I returned the same way, late in the afternoon, the kids were begging coins from passersby. They had brilliant smiles but were absolutely dirty and wearing rags. I noted that they hadn't started their begging duties until late in the afternoon as the working community undertook the evening rush hour. There was a red-light district just two blocks away, and it didn't take much imagination to understand that as the crowd of office workers going home disappeared, the kids would move on to beg from the arriving throng of night people. The night scene was made up of, for the most part, unsavory folks to say the least. Many of them were not the kind of adults for the kids to be around. I worried about the risk to the kids.

I came by the next morning and saw the kids were still there. For whatever reason, fate had presented me with their need. I had to find some help for them. As I went on to Mercy, I decided to ask for help from Mercy's Street Children Outreach team. This would be my first time to see them in action.

Later that day, Khun Samran, the leader of the street kids outreach team stopped by to tell me that he had sent two of his team to check on the kids and he had a report. The kids were there because their dad, an alcoholic, was one of the group living under the bridge. Their story was unfortunately a common enough one for street people in Bangkok. They had been on a farm in the northeast of the country, called Isan, and were tenant farmers. After a bad harvest, they were left without food or income, so the parents had decided to come to Bangkok to look for work. Living on the street became too much for their mother. She had broken down mentally and emotionally and just wandered off one day. After their mother left, their father, who had been a moderate drinker before, turned to alcohol full-time. The kids were begging on the street to support their father and themselves.

Khun Samran told me that a couple of guys from his team would be going down to talk with the kids at 10 a.m. the next morning and invited me to meet them there. I had no idea what the street-kids team would do and was happy at the chance to meet up with them and see how they might address the problem.

When I came down the next morning, I couldn't see the kids under the bridge. I went around the corner toward my usual motorbike stop and then saw the kids, with a couple of staff from the Mercy Centre, about twenty meters down an empty asphalt walkway that paralleled the train tracks.

I went down to them, introduced myself to the Mercy guys who were expecting me, and found the kids having a great time. The staff had met with their father, still hungover, under the bridge, and gotten his permission to talk with the kids away from the group of guys around them. First, they helped the kids to clean up. They had soap and water for the kids to wash their hands. Then they gave them toothbrushes and toothpaste to brush their teeth on the spot. That was followed by handing out some writing books and pencils and giving a writing lesson starting with the kid's names.

All the while, there was a very low-key questioning process going on. They needed to find out how the kids had ended up there and what their daily situation was like. It was impressive. The Mercy staff were professional in what had to be the best of professions, directly caring for kids in need.

The situation developed over the next several days, with two or more of the staff going down each morning. I was there a couple of times, took pictures, and talked to the kids just a bit. Their names were Fai, the twelve-year-old girl, and Khao, the ten-year-old boy. They were bright and engaged kids. After a few meetings, I went back to my regular work schedule at Mercy and about a week later got a follow-up report from Khun Samran. It had taken some time, but they had gotten permission from the kid's dad to bring them down to stay at Mercy and go to school with kids their age. It had taken a while because the Mercy staff had to take the father to the nearest police station, the Lumpini police, for the father to sign the papers. The police told Khun Samran the father was really sad to do it, but that he understood and accepted that it was necessary for the kid's welfare.

The kids were at Mercy and safe. I relaxed and went back to my job thinking I would catch up and visit them once they had become used to Mercy. Khun Samran paid me a visit after a week and told me the police had called to say the father had died. Basically, he had drunk himself to death.

That wasn't the end, however. The Mercy Home, no matter how much the staff try to make the kids comfortable, is still an institution. An institution with as many as 200 or so kids of all ages, and kids can be cruel. When the Mercy kids learned that Fai and Khao's father had died from drinking, a small group started to bully them about it. The bullying affected Fai so much that she threw herself off a third-story balcony at

Mercy. She survived but had a severe concussion from which she would never recover. Fai had to be sent to a state home and school for the handicapped. It was not expected she would ever regain her full senses.

The staff discouraged me from trying to visit her, citing her lack of awareness. "Khun Tom, she won't know who you are. She doesn't know who anyone is."

I have never stopped feeling guilty about our inability to protect a young girl we thought we were saving. In a discussion with Fr. Joe, his advice to me was, "Give the guilt to the angels. They will carry it for you." Fr. Joe does believe in angels. It was a healing thought, but somehow my angels haven't been able to shoulder the full burden.

Khao did well at Mercy. He stayed at Mercy and went through school finishing high school. We didn't really talk but I saw him several times to say hi. He is now about twenty-two, married, and has a job as a motorcycle pizza delivery guy. That's a real success for a Mercy kid. I hope to meet him after the Covid pandemic is over and give him and his bride a wedding present.

Chapter Seven

CHUCK & HELGA
2007–PRESENT

It was Christmas of 2007 at Mercy. I had undergone a knee operation a couple weeks before Christmas; thus, I wasn't traveling and was at my second home, Mercy, for the holidays. As Thailand is a Buddhist nation, celebrating the birth of Christ is not a big religious event. However, Christmas is a great excuse to go shopping and party in all Asian countries. The lights and commercial decorations in central Bangkok are on a par with any western country. It is definitely a festive time.

Fr. Joe decided to have a few of the Mercy staff in for dinner and drinks at his residence, and I was invited. Dinner at Fr. Joe's place was always a great treat. Several of the staff, headed by his executive secretary, Khun Ratana, would gather and group cook a Western meal, on this occasion a turkey and some traditional American side dishes. Also, Joe always had on hand a collection of very fine Tuscan wines thanks to Rossano, an Italian restauranteur friend of his in Bangkok.

I was moving slowly because of my knee operation but still managed to arrive a few minutes early that evening. Soon after walking in, I made excuses for my still sore and healing knee and sought refuge on one end of the sofa. Khun Nitaya (Dtai) came over and spoke with me, explaining that an older foreign couple who were strangers to Mercy might be joining us. She had met them the day before as they were wandering into the entrance to the Mercy courtyard.

They told Dtai they were just passing through town, had heard of Mercy, and wanted to see it. That was a bit unusual. Mercy, located in the middle of the slum, is not easy to get to. Usually, visitors don't come by unless they have a contact of some sort in Mercy. Dtai was polite and gave them a brief tour of Mercy, though Fr. Joe was not on hand to meet with them. The couple seemed to be all alone, so as they were leaving, Dtai told them about the coming dinner the next night and invited them to return for dinner with Fr. Joe and some of the staff. They accepted, but she wasn't sure they would be coming.

However, a few minutes after I had settled myself comfortably down on the sofa, there was a knock on the side door to Joe's residence. I heard Dtai and the security guard talking. The guard had the two visitors with him. Dtai showed the couple up the stairs and into the living/dining room area of the residence. The couple appeared to be in their seventies and Dtai took them around introducing them while I remained seated. Then the older gentleman, walking slowly, headed toward the sofa and sat down next to me. I apologized for not getting up to meet them and explained that I had just had a knee operation. He laughed and mentioned that he had had several knee operations, which was why he was moving slowly. Thus, I met Chuck Feeney. As we talked Fr. Joe put his wife, Helga, to work in the kitchen helping with the salad.

Chuck's demeanor was quite easy going and his attire very casual, to the point of being a bit disordered. As we talked, introducing ourselves, he gave away very little about himself. He was an American businessman and had traveled around the world many times. He and his wife had come to the habit, some years back, of spending Christmas time at the Laguna Beach resort in Phuket. As we spoke it became obvious to me, despite his somewhat disorderly attire and casual manner, this was a very bright man of substance. It occurred to me that I'd best let Fr. Joe know that these guests were not two accidental visitors. I excused myself and went over to Joe. He was busy directing the meal preparations which, as you might guess, really didn't need his attention. I grabbed his arm and told him, "I don't know exactly who he is, you just put his wife to work in the kitchen, but this is an important man. I don't think he's a casual visitor." Joe acknowledged that, went back to the food preparation orchestration, and we had a great dinner.

Thus, Chuck and Helga Feeney, the greatest friends Mercy could have, arrived on the scene. I learned over the following months that Chuck was not known to the world because he didn't want to be famous. He avoided the spotlight and publicity of any kind. It was just his nature. Chuck had made his fortune as one of the founders of Duty-Free Shops, which started at the airport in Hong Kong in the early 1960s and spread to airports throughout the world over the next thirty years. He was at one time the world's greatest philanthropist and had donated billions of dollars to charitable projects through his foundation, Atlantic Philanthropies. He started giving at a time, the early Eighties, when a billion dollars was still a lot of money. He eventually donated his entire fortune (which grew to over $8 billion) to the foundation he had started. His guideline was simple, "Giving While Living". Chuck's goal was that the foundation should disburse all the funds he had put into it, which would be all his fortune, prior to his death rather than the conventional idea that a philanthropist would donate some of his wealth after his death. Chuck's joke was that he wanted his "last check to bounce." The concept behind the idea was that money given now would have much more impact going forward than money given twenty or thirty years in the future.

I believe he was the inspiration for Bill Gates and Warren Buffet when they started the Giving Pledge in 2010. Chuck immediately signed the pledge. The Giving Pledge for billionaires is that they will pledge to donate the majority of their fortune while living. This is not as aggressive as Chuck Feeney's concept, but still a major ramping up of philanthropy for many of the world's richest people.

Chuck continued on the board of Atlantic Philanthropies as the founder, though he didn't act as chair. The board made the donations, which he voted on but didn't dictate. The board gave him a modest fund, about $50 million a year I believe, which he could direct for donations he found and favored in his travels. Helga Feeney told me later that the funds he actually directed could be greater. I came to understand, as Helga Feeney told me, that "He did not necessarily believe in budgets in his giving." He would do research on his own and find smaller charities or organizations, mostly medical, which he would propose to the board for their approval. An excellent book on Chuck, his life, and his philanthropy is *The Billionaire Who Wasn't*, by Conor O' Cleary.

Thus, Chuck's visit to Mercy was part of his personal charity research. Atlantic Philanthropies normally didn't direct donations to small organizations but looked for large donation possibilities to universities and hospitals for the most part. Chuck would find small charities that interested him through magazine or newspaper articles. I have in my mind's eye a picture of Chuck, his rumpled figure slumped in an airport chair somewhere waiting to board his flight. He would find an article he liked about a charity or hospital or medical need, carefully tear it out, fold it, and pass it on to one of his friends to check out. This was possibly not the most efficient method of routing his charitable donations, but Chuck's heart has certainly been in all of his giving.

Though born and raised in America, Chuck has a strong love for Ireland and, for many years, had contributed to charitable needs in Ireland. Fr. Joe was of Irish parentage on his mother's side, and he had always claimed that background. Newspaper reporters in Bangkok had been referring to Fr. Joe as the Irish-American priest since the 1990s. Thus, through what I came to refer to as the Irish connection, Chuck found his way to Mercy. I believe that a news story about Mercy, referring to Fr. Joe as the Irish-American slum priest, is how Chuck came to pick Mercy to visit. He had asked a close friend, Bob Matousek, to visit Mercy some months previously to see if Mercy would be worthy of consideration. Bob had reported back and told Chuck it would be worth his while to stop at Mercy on the next trip he and Helga made to Thailand.

Following the Christmas dinner, Chuck and Helga came back in the spring. Again, it was a normal part of their travel schedule. It should be noted here that in line with turning his back on the glitter that could be found in great wealth, Chuck always traveled in economy class when he could have easily owned the plane. Fr. Joe invited them to another dinner at his residence and introduced them to a friend of Mercy who spent much of the year in Thailand. This was the NYU professor and traditional Irish folk musician Mick Moloney. Chuck and Mick hit it off immediately. Mick asked around later and learned that behind the scenes, Chuck had funded much of the costs of the negotiations in Northern Ireland which led to the Good Friday Agreement of April 10, 1998, and that he was also a strong supporter and active in the funding of Limerick University, which happened to be in Mick's hometown. These were great accomplishments and Chuck had never said a word about it to us.

Chuck loved traditional Irish music, or "trad" music, as the Irish say. Mick performed some banjo and mandolin tunes after the dinner at Fr. Joe's, which started a discussion about a possible benefit concert for Mercy. At that time Chuck and Helga maintained a pied-à-terre in New York

City. Mick, who spent the fall school terms teaching a course at NYU, also had an apartment there. Mick knew the music scene of the city well. It was Mick's idea to work with the Irish Arts Center in New York and organize a charity concert for Mercy the following September. Chuck loved the idea and agreed to work with Mick in support of the concert. In the end, the concert was a smashing success and did indeed raise money for Mercy. Mick has gone on over the years to assemble groups of Irish and Irish-American musicians, all his friends, to hold concerts in the U.S. to raise funds for Mercy and other charities in Thailand.

The concert was wonderful, but the stories Mick came back with about Chuck and his approach to the project were fascinating. Mick had learned how Chuck had come to be a billionaire. One attribute was the fantastic attention to detail that Chuck bought to each matter. A concern he had was parking for the concert. He wanted to be sure that there were sufficient spaces in the parking buildings near the concert hall to accommodate the full attendance expected at the concert. He invited Mick along and, on foot, went through each of the parking buildings counting the spaces available and checking the cost. No detail was too small. When Chuck was involved, nothing was left to chance.

The timing of Chuck's arrival at Mercy couldn't have been better from our point of view. Though we had received record donations in the previous years following the tsunami, we had also set records for expenditures and still had promises to keep. It should be noted that Mercy is organized as an independent foundation, and not funded by the Catholic church. Mercy is dependent on public donations to sustain it's programs serving the poor. The problem we were facing as we went into 2008 was that while expecting diminishing donations over the coming years, we were still operating to some extent at much higher cost levels. The future was uncertain at best. As one who worked on the finances closely with the accountants, I was seriously concerned that Mercy would not be able to pay the bills and would be in danger of failing.

What happened after Chuck's visits to Mercy was pure Chuck Feeney. He again left the guidance Mercy would need to his friend Bob Matousek, who visited several weeks later and gave me the guidelines for a proposal to Atlantic Philanthropies. As you can imagine, we turned the proposal around very quickly. I learned later that Chuck had to argue a bit with the board as they thought a small donation such as he proposed for Mercy wasn't in line with the Atlantic Philanthropies charter.

Chuck prevailed. In December of 2008, we received $1 million, the first installment of a $3 million donation that would be given over the next three years. To put this into perspective, Chuck's donation was made after the stock market crash in September of 2008, during a time when Mercy's need was high and normal donations were going down quickly. His donation, and other direct assistance, kept Mercy afloat through 2011 as we worked to overcome the remaining costs of the tsunami effort and strived to develop a sustainable budget. It wasn't made public and few people, even inside Mercy, understood that Chuck had saved Mercy.

Chuck and Helga became good friends to Mercy on a personal basis over those years. When they came to Thailand at Christmas and in the spring of each year, they made a point of stopping in to see how we were progressing. Chuck invited a small group from Mercy to join him and Helga at the Laguna Beach hotel in Phuket. We learned then that he co-owned the hotel with a Thai partner. He told us the hotel would always be open to Mercy should we do further work in the south.

Mercy had received large donations in the past, specifically from people whose goal was to put up buildings with their names on them. We did need the buildings, but as I told Fr. Joe, the problem with the new buildings was that prospective donors would come down to Mercy, see the new buildings, and conclude we were rich and didn't need their support. I was subsequently to hear that phrase directly several times by people who turned away. "Tom, it looks like you guys are doing pretty good already." New buildings didn't help with our greatest need, which was operating funds.

The Thai have a saying, "to put your gold on the back of the Buddha." It comes from the Thai custom, when going to pray and make merit at temples, to take a further step and buy a one-inch square of gold, pounded as thin as could be, and paste it on the temple's Buddha statue. This results in many of the figures having a brilliant gold exterior. Most people would paste the square of gold on the front and have their picture taken with the Buddha image. Making merit in pasting the gold on the back of the figure, without putting yourself in front, was an act of self-effacement that came to be known as "putting your gold on the back of the Buddha."

Chuck understood and practiced that way of giving. It was part of his ethos. Without publicity or putting his name on anything, he made sure we had the money to survive at a difficult time. Also, beyond his foundation's donation, he would work directly, as he did at the concert, to assist our general fundraising down the road. He stood out in his commitment to Mercy even while maintaining that it must be his usual behind-the-scenes effort.

As I write this Chuck has succeeded in giving away his fortune. Chuck signed the papers to close down Atlantic Philanthropies in September of 2020. He retained some modest funds to live on. As the Irish say, Chuck is a mighty man. Chuck and Helga now reside in San Francisco as their choice of a retirement city. My wife and I still have the pleasure of meeting them for lunch when we pass through.

God bless you, Chuck and Helga.

The Sleepy Boy—Od

Many times, a child would come to my attention as I sat at the entranceway to the Mercy Centre. There were two benches set just inside, facing out to the street. It was a good place to sit as people came to visit or the kids came back from school. Oft-times, after work in the late afternoon, I would go there and sit and just watch the Mercy world unfolding about me and try to absorb it a bit. I knew the finance work was important, in its place, but the homes were the real Mercy. As I sat there the AIDS ward was on my far-right side, the community aid office to my immediate right, and the overall aid office on my left side. Many times, I would find Fr. Joe sitting there and I could say hi and catch up with how he was feeling about things. Joe loves to gossip about what is new at Mercy. Other staff and some of the kids would stop by at times.

One afternoon one of the Mercy Homes staff was there with a young boy, possibly eight years old. He was sitting next to her, leaning against her, and looked half asleep. I said hi and asked who the boy was as I hadn't seen him before. She said he was a new boy who had been dropped off at the Mercy entrance a week or two before. To the question of who had dropped him off and why, there was no answer. It was possible that he had been with a gang of street kids and that they had just dropped him off to get a meal. Of course, the Mercy staff had taken him in, fed him, and put him to stay with the boys his age. They were trying to get him started in school, but she told me the problem was that he was very lazy. They didn't know what to do with him. He was always falling asleep.

As I looked at him, I could see he was low-energy, but I felt somehow it wasn't lazy. His height and weight seemed normal for his age. His eyes were aware. I asked the staffer if there was a medical problem. She said not as far as they knew. He ate his meals and went around normally at times but very often would fall asleep. He was just lazy.

I said hello to the boy—his name was Od—and then goodbye to the staff member and went on home. In the taxi on my way back home, I couldn't stop thinking about it. In my experience, kids his age were not lazy. They ran like crazy instead, asked questions, made trouble. Overactive was normal, but not lazy. One problem was that though there was a government medical care facility in the slums, hospital number 44 I think, it was pretty much limited to trauma or severe, relatively easy-to-diagnose things, such as TB or cancerous growths. Anything that was relatively hidden could stay hidden.

The next day I asked the staff if they had taken the boy to a doctor or the hospital to have him examined. The answer was no. In a way, it was a foolish question. Mercy was not a place for next-level medical care, people in the slum didn't see doctors unless they had something that shouted for attention. I spoke with Khun Usannee, our executive director and chief medical person, and asked if she would mind if I took Od to the hospital to get him checked. She said it was okay and mentioned to me that Sr. Joan, an Australian nun who worked in the slum with expectant and new mothers, was planning on taking a young girl that she had come across in her rounds to the hospital. Possibly we could go together.

It should be noted that Sr. Joan is herself a remarkable story. She had served as a school principal at a Catholic girl's school near Perth, Australia. When she came to the age of sixty and decided against retirement, she said her next job should be as a missionary working with the poor in the Klong Toey slum area in Bangkok. She arrived in Klong Toey in 1991. While not directly working for Mercy, she was, as the communists would say, a fellow traveler. Despite her age, she never let the heat, dirt, or physical demands of delivering milk formula supplements and counseling the young slum moms stop her rounds. She was a friend and I admired her greatly.

I phoned Sr. Joan and she told me she had a plan to go to the children's hospital the next morning and she would be happy to have

Od and me join with her and the young girl. Sr. Joan had taken children to this hospital several times. This would be my first trip. I let Khun Usanee know, and she arranged for Od and me to meet at Mercy the next morning to join up with Sr. Joan.

From Mercy, Sr. Joan, the two kids, and I shared a taxi to the Children's Hospital in central Bangkok. This was an older government hospital, so it was a grey concrete building, definitely plain in appearance. The inside was also very government, featuring government-issue furniture and somewhat dingy light brown walls. Possibly it was meant to be soothing, which, in a way, it was. *Don't expect too much.* There was a small crowd, but we had only a fifteen-minute wait in the line to be directed to a doctor's office. I held Od's hand and steered him along. He was nervous and looking around but definitely passive.

This was where we parted with Sr. Joan and the child she was caring for. They were designated for a different area of the hospital. Now the adventure would start. We agreed to meet back at Mercy as there was no telling how long it would take and what differing schedules we might be following.

I found the nurse's desk in our area and presented Od and myself to her. This was one of those times when racial prejudice worked in Od's favor. Because he was with a white man, it was assumed he was important. We didn't jump the queue, but the nurse made sure to let us know we would be seen as soon as possible and asked us to have a seat on a brown wood bench against the brown wall. It was slow.

After thirty minutes, she came to get Od. She told me I had to wait, that the doctor would talk to Od alone. Od was in with the doctor for another twenty minutes, and then they brought him out to me. The nurse told me they had taken some blood samples and sent them off to be tested in another area of the hospital. She asked me to be patient and said it would take at least an hour.

The waiting was what it is in hospitals. It was not too busy and there wasn't much noise from the other children walking around and talking with their parents, all moms except for me. There was a big clock on the wall ticking out the minutes in hospital time, slow and slower. Od was awake and remained passive. He wriggled now and then but just remained quiet next to me. Sr. Joan came by and told me she and the young girl were going to see a second doctor, a specialist. To my shame, I cannot remember what the girl's problem was. I was focused on Od.

Finally, the doctor came back out and told me he had the test results. He had anticipated them. What he told me was a bit troubling. He said the medical problem was a blood disease called Thalassemia, which caused constant fatigue. It was actually one that had a variation unique to the Thai DNA in some way and was found more frequently in the southern Thailand population than elsewhere in the world. He told me that otherwise, Od was a normal, healthy, intelligent boy and that the problem was manageable. He gave me a prescription and directed me to the hospital pharmacy to have it filled and pay the bill. I can't remember the exact amount, but Thai government hospitals are not expensive.

When we got out on the street to catch a taxi, I noticed an ice cream stand across the street. I asked Od if he would like some ice cream and, of course, he did. We went over and got the ice cream, which he started working on, and I looked to wave down a cab. He soon finished the ice cream cone and a cab appeared. We got in and set off on the ride back to Mercy, it was, as always, a negotiation with the taxi driver: drivers never wanted to go to the Jet Sip Rai slum. Od settled in next to me, and after about ten minutes, he was propped against me and fell sound asleep. It brought out all the protective parental instincts in me.

As we drove on, the taxi route went directly by my apartment in Bangkok. I wanted to tell the driver to stop. My thought was to take Od home and make sure he would be all right. Of course, that wasn't possible. Besides the reality that any decision would have to involve my wife, it wasn't the way Mercy did things. He probably had family. They needed to be looked for. Mercy had professional staff to do the job, not me.

At Mercy, I found the staff member I had talked with and turned Od over to her. I made sure she understood that Od was sick and gave her the medicine the doctor had prescribed and directions on when to take it. She told me Od would be sent back to school. As I left, once again I had some hope that I had been able to help a Mercy kid. It was not to be.

A few days later I went to check on how Od was doing. He wasn't around. A staff member told me Od was gone. "Just gone" wasn't enough, I needed a more adequate answer. I went to see Khun Samran of the street kids outreach program, my most reliable source and advisor. He was aware of what had happened. He mentioned again that it was thought that Od had been dropped off at Mercy by a street kids gang. Now it seemed that the gang had just stopped by again, told him to come along, and Od had gone off with them.

I was devastated. I explained to Samran about the doctor's exam results and the need for Od to take his medication. Samran understood. He told me that his teams would be looking for Od at the differing street kid collection points they visited each day and night. I asked him for ideas on possible locations as I was determined to look around myself at nights after work.

Over the next few weeks, I searched and searched, looking over any group of kids I might see, with no result. It was terribly frustrating, but I felt I had to do something. After a couple of weeks, neither Samran's staff nor I were able to find him. He was gone into the night. No meds. No hope. Unfortunately, the reality of losing some of the street kids was part of life at Mercy and I'm sure other street kid's organizations. Samran was sympathetic to me and appreciated that I had tried, but also his expression told me, this is sometimes the way it is. I had to accept it.

To explain how Od could be visited by kids from outside Mercy and then simply walk out, one must understand that Mercy is not a jail. It's a home. While the kids are encouraged to stay, go to school, and be safe, there are no bars on the windows or extensive security to keep kids inside. There is never enough staff to watch over two hundred kids constantly.

Also, life on the streets can be attractive to kids with no home or immediate family. Usually, the street gangs are older, not Od's age. Once kids on the street get to be old enough to forage for themselves, twelve or thirteen, it's very hard to get them to come in and accept the boring routine of being school kids. As difficult as life can be on the streets, they feel free, and that is a powerful force. It was also possible that there was an older boy looking out for Od. For me, it was again a lesson in the reality of life at Mercy. It was not a fault of Mercy, but rather the reality of life in a slum and for the kids born into it. The fact that Od would struggle mightily without his medication was just more painful reality.

Vietnam—February 1967—Not Present for Duty

The language of the military report is dry and limited. "Operational Report—Lessons Learned", written by the 25th Infantry Division in

October 1967, covering the February 1 through April 30, 1967 quarter, describes the action as follows:

"On 22nd February, Alpha Company of the 4th Battalion 9th Inf. Regiment was dispatched to the Filhol rubber plantation to clear the road from Cu Chi to the village of Phu Hoa Dong, and to provide security for Engineer elements clearing the wooded area. On the 26th of February, at 0030, Alpha Company, was attacked by an estimated Viet Cong (VC) battalion using mortars, rifle grenades and human wave assault tactics. The attack was repelled by AW (automatic weapons) artillery, gunships and air strikes. Action terminated at 0800 hours. There was no further contact in February."

In later pages, the report noted that with regard to item (c) Ice Cream, an issue was made every other day to troops at Cu Chi base with 1,477 gallons per week coming from Saigon and 903 gallons a week manufactured in Cu Chi.

After ice cream, in the section giving a review of division strength, the report cited 116 officers and men killed in action (KIA) during the period, and 1,239 wounded in action (WIA). That is about as impersonal as you can get, but of course a modern army must track all the numbers, both ice cream and KIAs. But, for me, there was one important number missing.

One particular soldier was not present for duty on 26th February 1967. Alpha Company was my company. Twenty-six men of my company were killed in action and another forty wounded, and I was not there to help. I was absent from duty, still in the hospital in Japan. That failure to be on hand when I was needed has haunted me all my life.

The way I learned of the fight was through the hospital grapevine. Someone approached me, knowing I was assigned to the 25th Infantry Division, and let me know that a new batch of wounded had come in from Vietnam. A number of 25th Infantry soldiers were included. I didn't know any of them personally, but when I went to talk with them, they told me it was Alpha Company that had taken the majority of the casualties. For me, the news was a ticket to hell. I was sick, dumbfounded, and fell into the blackest depression. I had let the troops down. I should have been there. I should have died with them. Nothing else was acceptable.

In an action unusual for me, I went to the hospital chapel and prayed to understand. This was a significant move for me as I had not gone to church in years. The hospital chapel was used for services by all denominations and was spare in its decoration and layout. That was best for me. I just wanted a place where I could examine what had happened and what it meant. Where I could focus on the lives of those who had died and, in doing so, struggle to gain my own spiritual grip on its meaning. I visited several times over the period of a few days, some of the sessions lasting an hour or more. I won't go through the many thoughts I considered, except to say that at the end, I wasn't mourning for the death of my men alone but for the deaths of all those involved in the battle. I'll leave it there.

The men who died were not looking for military glory or career advancement, but rather young men who just sought to support the soldiers they served with, serve their country, and do their duty to the best of their ability.

Amongst seven soldiers from my platoon, the list included another of my squad leaders, Sergeant Ray Nixon, a skinny man, only five foot six inches tall, who spoke to me of walking through rice paddies as a soldier in Korea in 1952 and then wondered what the hell he was doing walking through rice paddies again in Vietnam in 1966. Sergeant Nixon died after getting out of his foxhole during the most intense phase of the February 26 battle, running to the rear for ammunition for his troops and on his return being killed by the enemy after exposing himself to their fire in a heroic manner. I'm sure he would have said he was just doing his job. The list would include Spec. 4 Bob Carnoske, my RTO, who once showed me his favorite picture from home in St. Louis, a 1957 Chevy, clean and beautiful. After I went to the hospital in Japan, he was promoted to a presumably safer position as the company commander's RTO, only to be killed when the VC made assaulting the command post a key part of the attack on the company position. There are many more. I keep their names and go over them and think of them often, and will until I die, wishing I had been a better soldier serving with them.

There were names I didn't find as some of the soldiers I had known, including my trustworthy Sergeant Amado, had rotated out of Vietnam in the weeks of my absence and been replaced by new troopers.

It was too late to be any use, but I went to the doctors and persuaded them to agree that I could return immediately to Vietnam and my unit.

The plane ride back to Saigon from Yokota airbase outside of Tokyo was in total contrast to my initial flight to Vietnam six months earlier.

There was no chatter at all. Everyone on the flight had been wounded in combat and knew what they were returning to. We all settled into our own wells of silence, wrapped in blankets to combat the overactive air conditioning on the plane. It was a long, cold, dark flight. The beast of war was waiting, and we all understood it was completely chance whether we would survive or not. My thinking was very clear. I needed to get back on the line and do what I had been trained to do and was confident I could do. I didn't have a death wish, but I was ready to accept whatever might come in order to redeem myself.

Chapter Eight

A GOVERNMENT
VISITOR—2008

Mercy had received little official attention from U.S. government personnel over the years. Occasionally there would be a staff member at the U.S. embassy who had been raised Catholic, and out of personal interest and a desire to meet the American priest who became known for his work with Mercy, decided they wanted to come down to introduce themselves and learn something of Mercy. Over the years these included some high-level staff such as the Political-Military Counselor, Matt Daley in the 1980s, and Ambassador Eric John in 2008.

The request we received from the embassy, in a hand-delivered letter in late July of 2008, was of much greater import. Mercy had been selected to be the occasion for that most sacred of political events, a photo op. Of course, that was not what it stated in the letter, rather just that President George Bush and Mrs. Bush would be coming to Thailand for a brief visit in early August. As Mercy was a charitable foundation headed by an American priest, Mercy was being considered a newsworthy stop.

The clamor this request aroused in Mercy was enormous. Khun Usanee called a meeting to discuss the letter. She, by then, had been given the title of executive director of Mercy. Supposedly that meant she would receive staff reports and make management decisions to ease Fr. Joe's work burden, which she did. However, this was a difficult management task. Fr. Joe would jump into the decision chain whenever he felt the urge.

This time, Fr. Joe didn't lead the discussion. Khun Usannee did,

showing the letter to the staff and announcing that we had been picked
by the embassy for a visit by President Bush. Maybe, that is. It was
explained that the President's plans were still not firm, but we should do
what we could to prepare for the visit in any case. Staff members from
the embassy and the President's advance party would come down the
next day to inspect Mercy.

It was clear that nobody knew what to do, including Fr. Joe. He had
met with embassy representatives over the years, several of whom were
enthusiastic about Mercy, but he felt that on a normal basis, the embassy
staff did little for Mercy. That day, he seemed a bit unenthusiastic about
how to proceed. One normally doesn't say no to the President of the
United States. Khun Usanee saw the confusion in the room and then
asked what I thought. To me, it was a no-brainer. The visit would provide
a journalistic boost in awareness of Mercy's presence and hopefully for
our fundraising. I made that point and then confessed that I had worked
on a Presidential visit years before when I served as a foreign service
officer in the U.S. embassy in Seoul, Korea. I saw some relief on Khun
Usanee's face, but the staff and Fr. Joe still seemed uncertain. Sr. Maria
was not in the meeting, but when it was all explained to her later, she
had no interest. She had work to do and no time to be involved. She
was not impressed.

Khun Usanee ended the meeting by suggesting a small group of
senior staff meet with the embassy representatives the next day in the
Mercy conference room to plan the visit. She and I would discuss who
and how after the meeting. Of course, Fr. Joe would be on hand to be
introduced to the visitors.

It seems that serving on a Presidential staff can be a heady experience.
You represent power. Even if you have little power of your own, you are
speaking for whoever owns the throne. In my experience, sometimes
senior U.S. government folks could be overbearing.

The two very young, maybe just out of college, girls who appeared at
Mercy the next afternoon were both a bit overly authoritative and a bit
naïve. When they arrived, over thirty minutes late, they quickly made it
clear that they were in charge and that they expected a complete response
to the guidelines we were to be given for the visit.

It hit me that it was the President's lame-duck year. My thought
was that these two young girls from Texas had been given graduation
jobs at the White House as a political favor to their parents. They were

excited, enthusiastic, but not on a level with the professional White House advance people I had met in my previous experience working in the U.S. embassy in Seoul. They were accompanied by a lady, a mid-level embassy staffer, who seemed a bit embarrassed by the overly pushy manner of the two Presidential advance staffers. She caught my eye and just nodded. The girls were in charge, not her.

The girls, of course, did not speak Thai. We introduced them to Fr. Joe. who was not amused with their youthful manner but held his tongue for the moment. After his introduction, he turned to Khun Usanee and me and said that we would handle the preparations for the visit and walked out. Good move. The girls gave some guidelines that I knew came from the Secret Service advance team. They wanted the names and ID information of all the Mercy staff who would be on hand for the visit. Only those on the approved list could be at Mercy at the time of the visit. They also said that the number should be limited. The Mercy Centre main building would be closed to all other staff and visitors.

Main Mercy was a three-story building that at that time included the offices of the community aid staff, a meeting room, the thirty beds of the AIDS hospice on the first and second floors, an arts shop on the first floor, and a computer room. Fr. Joe's residence and a three-story preschool were adjacent to the offices. It was left to Khun Usanee and me to make a plan for the President's tour. The advance team girls would be back the next day at the same time to review the plan, check the list of attendees, and do a walkthrough. I wondered if "the same time" meant they would be thirty minutes late again but didn't ask the question. Then, still bustling with import and excitement, they hurried on their way.

One of the keystone elements of Thai social behavior is the respect required of the younger person for the older. The pee-nong (older-younger) precept is so strong that even a difference of just a few years, such as between a person of thirty and one of thirty-five, would cause the older person to expect some clear deference from the younger. Also, a calm demeanor in social interactions was highly valued and expected. To say these two youngsters had just shattered some Thai social standards would be a vast understatement.

The Mercy group was left stunned. After the advance team had left they looked at each other in wonderment, they looked at Khun Usanee, they looked at me. What should we do? This meeting had been a very unpleasant experience and one beyond their understanding.

Khun Usanee asked us all to sit down and then looked at me. I could tell she would just as soon call the whole thing off. "Khun Tom, what should we do?"

I explained that though I felt the advance team girls had been a bit extreme, this was the way Presidential visits went. I warned her it would get worse. The Secret Service would be directly involved at a later stage and swarming about during the President's visit. They would not be delicate. It wasn't in their job description. Then we just sat down and worked out a plan as we had been asked to.

The next day we had a plan for showing the President through Mercy's main building after his meeting with Fr. Joe and the principal staff in the conference room. We met at the office in the main Mercy building and waited for the advance team. The girls were missing. The lady from the embassy was on hand but had no idea where the girls were. They had let her know they had important things to do and would meet her at Mercy. We waited, thirty minutes, forty-five minutes, and over an hour. Then the girls appeared, looking a bit flustered.

They had gone to meet a senior member of the advance team who was arriving at the airport earlier in the day. Only they hadn't realized that Bangkok had two airports. And the taxi driver, when they just told him to take them to the airport, had taken them to Don Muang, Bangkok's domestic airport. Disaster. They learned that the international airport was on the other side of town, a good hour's drive away. They jumped into another taxi and went over to Suvarnabhumi, Bangkok's international airport where they found the senior member of the advance team stewing and waiting for them. Then they had to ride back to what is now the St. Regis hotel with him, briefing him along the way. Then they jumped into another taxi and goodness, here we are! Wow. Isn't working at the top levels of government exciting?

The meeting could only go up from there. We shared with them our ideas for the walkthrough. The girls advised us that the President would be coming in through Mercy's back entrance as directed by the Secret Service. Okay, we rearranged the walkthrough to adapt to that. Also, we were advised that we would need a have a second practice walkthrough the next day. A Secret Service agent would be on hand to okay the people involved and the route and provide guidance. Don't touch the President. Speak only when spoken to. Et cetera.

The walkthrough with the Secret Service agent went off well if in a bit of a strained atmosphere. It was the agent's job to make sure all those who would be on-site knew that this was deadly serious business. He did his job, and it was a grim group of Mercy staff he left behind.

The day of the visit was chaos from our point of view. The Thai press had learned of the visit and formed a jostling mob at the front entrance of Mercy. We had numerous phone calls from occasional friends and contacts begging access, including one very persistent and demanding foreign journalist who considered herself a friend of Mercy. She had one of our staff in tears with her demands.

We had been told to keep out all of the Mercy office staff for the period of the visit. It would just be Fr. Joe, Khun Usanee, four senior managers, and me. The nurses at the AIDS hospice as well as the patients were allowed to remain.

The entourage and the Presidential limo arrived on time the next morning, using the back gate to Mercy to avoid the crowd of journalists. The local people didn't gather around, even though the limo and escort vehicles were an incredible attraction in the slum. The sight of the stern Secret Service agents surrounding the Presidential parade and security vehicles kept them distant. I learned later, from one of the staff, that the Secret Service had stationed a sniper on the roof of a nearby house. The Mercy staff member was a gun enthusiast and was absolutely delighted with that move. This was incredible theater for the Jet Sip Rai slum population.

A tentlike structure had been erected just outside Mercy's back door so the President could exit the car and enter Mercy under cover. As he entered, he came into a courtyard between the school and Fr. Joe's residence. The school had arranged for a group of the youngsters (all preschool students, remember) to be in formation to sing some songs for George. He seemed charmed and stopped to hear them out. While that was happening, one of the President's staff came up to me. He needed to find a site to set up communications equipment where some of the staff could be stationed during the visit. I told him that they could use Fr. Joe's residence. As the group walked toward the house guided by one of our staff, I could see one man carrying a fat briefcase. This was the "football", the nuclear weapons communications device. I admit, I only knew this because in the early 1980s, a marine officer friend of mine had held that job at the White House during part of President Reagan's term.

Fr. Joe, the staff, and I were standing in the conference room, just a few feet away from the school courtyard. A Secret Service agent came in, looked around, went over to the next rooms, looked around, and came back and nodded to the entourage. *It's okay to come in.*

My role was quite limited. I had been put on one side of the open-door entrance which was on my left and Fr. Joe and the senior staff were lined up opposite me with the door to their right. The President came through the door, and that was the start of the adventure. He paused for a second, turning to me. I then learned a lesson in presidential management. I nodded to him and, holding my hand waist-high, pointed in the opposite direction toward Fr. Joe and the staff. He reversed course, without hesitation, and walked toward the group holding his hand out to Fr. Joe. It seems presidents are very used to being managed. Just point a finger.

After staff introductions, the tour began. Khun Usanee was to lead the parade. Besides Fr. Joe, myself, and the Mercy staff, three of the President's men, including Chief of Staff Joshua Bolten, were along. The American ambassador, Eric John, was also in attendance. Of course, a number of Secret Service agents circled constantly, on the lookout for a possibly wayward child, I suppose. I walked just behind the President and Khun Usanee. Fr. Joe and the chief of staff were next to me. I had an unobstructed view.

The tour veered slightly off-balance from the start. As Khun Usanee explained the surroundings and Mercy's mission, the President, possibly to hear better, put an arm around Khun Usanee's shoulder. I presume this cozy approach was a normal and possibly welcome touch for women in Texas, but in Thailand, you never touch a woman in public. Even husband and wife normally keep their distance. However, Khun Usanee was a world traveler. She understood that the President marched to the beat of a different drum, and she just marched on.

We came to the AIDS ward. Remember, with fans used for ventilation purposes, the ward was open with large sliding glass doors, allowing a full view of the patients and nurses. The patients were in the beds and open to view from the walkway. It was close enough to see fully inside, but we had been told the President wouldn't enter the ward. I doubt it was in his experience. No telling what danger awaited. As they stood there with Khun Usanee, the originator of the Mercy AIDS program, giving a summary of its activities, the President was not paying full attention to the briefing.

With his arm still around her shoulder, George leaned his head a bit toward Khun Usanee and asked her, "Are you married?"

"Yes."

Then he asked her, "How much money does your husband make?"

"Not enough."

Bravo, Khun Usanee. Okay, time to move on.

We came next to the art room. This has been an important stopping point for visitors to Mercy over the years, as we had found that it was a chance for visitors (potential donors) to connect with the kids who used the room. It gives visitors a chance to see the artwork and talk with the kids, even if it's just to ooh and aah about the drawings. The President, knowing a photo op when he saw it, immediately sat down on one of the kid's chairs and talked to Keng, eight or nine years old at that time. Keng was an AIDS boy and one of the best artists. We translated for them. It was a nice moment. Keng was proud a foreigner would take time with him and his drawings. To give the President credit, I felt that he also valued the moment, and he handled himself well.

All the time, of course, the Presidential photographer was circling and snapping pictures. The result was that Keng and President Bush were pictured on the front page of the *Bangkok Post* the next day. I still have a copy of that edition of the paper and the picture the White House staff sent back to us. It is a great photo. When I look at it, it brings me instantly back to the moment. It was a great takeaway from the visit.

Thus, the tour came to an end in the allotted thirty minutes. As we filed out, I spoke with the chief of staff. He very kindly gave me his card and invited, sincerely I believe, the Mercy staff to visit the White House as his guests when we might next be in Washington D.C. I asked him what other events the President had on his schedule. He told me that the Mercy visit was the last for Thailand. They were leaving to go to Beijing that evening. Then, as the British say, the penny dropped.

The Summer Olympics in Beijing had just started. It was a lame-duck year. Why not schedule a visit to meet the rest of the Bush family at the Olympics and use an Asian tour as cover? Thailand and Mercy were just convenient stops along the way. Okay. I thought the visit to Mercy was great, and who should tell a president he can't go to the Olympics? Not me.

President Bush wasn't the only high-ranking visitor to Mercy over the years. We had a visit from a former Thai Prime Minister, Anand

Panyarachun, several years earlier. More recently, we've had Jesse Jackson, a princess from Bhutan and a chieftain of the Lakota Sioux. Over the years, a number of entertainers of note had also stopped by to take advantage of a good public relations opportunity, among them Richard Gere and Sting. Of much more import in Thailand, we had Thai royalty take an interest in Mercy at one time. The prince and heir apparent had married a lady of what was termed a common background. To provide her with activities worthy of the royal household, it was decided she should become a patron of certain charities. Thus, the Mercy Centre was chosen to receive royal patronage. This status didn't include any donation but did elevate the view of a charity among certain members of Thai society and business. As part of this process, Khun Usanee met with the princess several times and gave her tours of Mercy. Usanee said afterward that the princess was a charming, intelligent lady. Unfortunately, the prince, after a while, tired of the charming, intelligent lady. She lost her position, and the Mercy Centre lost its patron. That, though, is a story for another time.

There was an accidental and somewhat damaging result for Mercy from the visit. September 30 was less then two months away from the President's visit. The date is the end of the U.S. government's fiscal year. It was time to spend any budget money left sloshing around in the governmental coffers. The President remarked to Ambassador John, in front of Fr. Joe and Khun Usanee, that he understood that the U.S. Agency for International Development (USAID) in Thailand had over $3 million of aid funds left in their budget for the year. He asked Ambassador John, "These are good folks. Why can't some of that money be given to Mercy?" A nice thought. An innocent question. However, the handling of it became a problem for Mercy.

The press mob was still at the front entrance to Mercy after the President left. They wanted a statement. A senior Mercy staff member, with no experience addressing the piranhas of the press corps, was put out to speak to the press. What followed was not his fault. You can't put a freshman in front of a swarm of reporters hungry for a lead for their report.

They asked him, "How much money is the President going to give to Mercy?"

The only sane answer would be to ignore the question or to say none. Our staffer foolishly recounted the statement that the USAID had $3 million and some of it would possibly be given to Mercy. Well, what the press corps heard, all they wanted to hear, were the words $3 million.

The next day it was in all the newspapers that the President gave $3 million to Mercy. In the end, as I remember it, we did get a donation of about one percent of the advertised amount. Quite nice. Thank you. This erroneous press report would only add to the image problem Mercy had in terms of our fundraising. After that, potential donors would remark to me that they heard we were pretty set and turn away from making a donation.

Early on during my time at Mercy, Joe had asked me to substitute for him to go to a dinner and receive a donation from a Bangkok businessmen's ice hockey group, the Flying Farangs (farang being the Thai word for *foreigner)*. I asked him how he wanted me to respond. His direction was simple. We are always humbly grateful. So I was, and thus, I was well accepted. It should be noted that to this day, the Flying Farangs dedicate the returns from their major hockey event in Bangkok to Mercy, and to honor Fr. Joe. He is humbly grateful.

A final, sad, note is that over ten years later, Keng was to die of complications due to AIDS. He was a beautiful, joyous boy. I will always remember him. When President Bush toured Mercy, the arts and crafts program was under the direction of a staff lady named Auntie Phut, who hosted the visitors. She oversaw the program when I first came to Mercy in 1998. Over the years she was responsible for much of the artistic success of the children and contributed many pieces of artwork herself. Auntie Phut died this past year. She was a gentle, beautiful soul and much loved by all the Mercy staff and kids.

The Charming Rascal, Sweet Sixteen—Joop Chang

There are those, especially kids, who somehow manage to charm everyone they come in contact with. Joop Chang was one such girl. Her name, Joop Chang, meant *seashell,* specifically the type of seashell with a pointed bottom spiraling up to an open top, somewhat like an ice cream cone. Joop was one of what Fr. Joe referred to at times as the AIDS brigade. He used that term, I think, because when receiving their twice a day collection of before meal pills at 6 a.m. and 6 p.m. and exactly on time, they would be lined up like a bunch of troops before the nurse's window.

Joop had been living with her aunt for a number of years, and then the aunt said she couldn't care for her any longer. She was in her early teens when she came to Mercy, and she was the oldest of the kids in the AIDS brigade at that time. She had been living untreated much longer than the younger kids. So Joop was an older sister and a leader. However, she was quite sick when she came in, and even though the staff put her on the right meds and worked with her, they all knew, and possibly Joop knew, that it was only a matter of a few years until her body would give in to the illness.

Joop was sick enough that she was in bed or only able to walk around Mercy much of the time. When volunteers or visitors came through Mercy and found Joop, she always had a big smile. The smile was a bit lopsided, which made it even more charming. Plus, coming from her thin, frail frame, it was always a surprise. Most of the kids would give a shy smile, but there was nothing shy about Joop. She wanted to talk. She wanted attention and she got it. Whether she was meeting the Mercy staff, volunteers, or the occasional visitors, she would charm them. Fr. Joe was so taken with Joop that he would, at times, guide visitors to the AIDS ward to see the "star" patient.

Joop was a bright girl, and over time, she would learn to use her star power to her benefit. A good example, at the time, was her interaction with an outstanding Canadian volunteer, Mary McLean. Mary was in charge of the informal music program and, on one occasion, stopped by to visit Joop and entertain her by playing the guitar. Joop loved it and asked Mary for a guitar. She wanted to learn how to play. Mary did find an inexpensive guitar for Joop and presented it to her. It became apparent on follow-up visits that being able to play the guitar wasn't really Joop's goal. Her goal was to get more attention. What the lovable kid wanted was to be loved, and the charm show was her effort to get it.

You could say all kids want to be loved and try to attract attention, but young Joop was very accomplished in that regard. Besides gaining the attention of many of the staff, there wasn't a volunteer who didn't make the excursion to Joop's bedside or to catch her as she patrolled around Mercy. Mercy volunteers Tew Bunnag, John Padorr, and Mary McLean were regulars.

In between the work and frustration, there were golden moments at Mercy. One of those special moments involved the AIDS brigade. Two frequent visitors, Mick Moloney, a noted Irish musician who played the mandolin, and his good friend John Murphy, who performed magically on the uilleann pipes, were often there to serenade the AIDS kids to sleep at night. It was lovely to see how their music soothed the sickest of kids. Joop was always on their list of stops.

John MacTaggart, a volunteer and Bangkok resident who worked in the medical equipment field, was a frequent visitor and stalwart supporter of the AIDS ward and Joop. Joop also had overseas visitors, journalists, a couple of filmmakers who would find their way to Joop and others. We even had a relatively young, blond baroness from Germany whose father was a Mercy donor. The baroness was introduced to Joop and, when Joop learned that this visitor was considered royalty, she was over the moon. She equated royalty to being a princess and Joop wanted to have a princess for a friend. Joop, with the help of the volunteers, wrote some letters in English and tried to strike up a correspondence with the baroness after she departed to return to Europe. Unfortunately, as with many visitors, the baroness wasn't able to respond once she returned home. Joop was quite disappointed.

Initially, Joop responded to the care she received at Mercy. This consisted primarily of a good diet and the correct meds, provided to Mercy free of charge by the government. She was not able to go to school, however. She was too weak, her AIDS was in the advanced stages.

Over time, Joop started periodic visits to the nearby Klueynamthai hospital. It was not advanced, but it would take the poor, and the doctors knew Mercy. Of course, the poor always ended up in an open, quite bleak ward setting of twelve or sixteen beds in an open space that resembled a parking garage more than a hospital ward. The hospital didn't advertise AIDS treatment. What hospital would? The care Joop received was aimed primarily at her increased difficulties in breathing, as the hospital would hook her up to an oxygen tank and ensure she was on the correct AIDS medicines and that she took them fully and on time.

As time passed, Joop began to need more frequent stays in the hospital. I told her I would stop by and visit her. The best time to visit was on a weekend. I would go on a Sunday morning. Joop loved all such visits. I would ask her what she wanted, and she would recite a list of candies she felt she was in need of. I understood it would be better if she didn't have too many sweets, but I felt my visits amounted to just an "occasional" indulgence. I would run down to the 7-Eleven convenience store on the ground floor and come back with a small stock of the most desirable items. Joop was delighted, as she was when any one of her vassals performed well.

Between Joop's lack of English and my rudimentary Thai, we sometimes struggled to make proper connections on filling her needs. I remember one visit at Mercy when Joop was making it clear she wanted something, but I wasn't quite sure what. Then I asked Joop what the special occasion was, thinking I really should have some limits when it came to running for the items she wanted. It was understood I was a committed vassal, but I felt I couldn't be a lackey. She said it was for her birthday. Well, she had me trumped. I couldn't say no to a birthday wish. So we discussed what month and what day. The day was easily determined but I wasn't clear on what month when she said it. I prompted her, asking if it was the current month, July, or Karackada in Thai. She paused, looked at me for a second, and then with a delighted smile said yes, yes, it's this month, Karackada. What would she like? Some jewelry. The coming birthday would be Joop's sixteenth. I guess she felt it was time for a more adult gift.

It seems to me that there is nothing worse than a guy shopping for women's jewelry, but I had to try. I asked several of the women on the Mercy staff for advice and finally decided on a neck chain with a small emblem. At the conclusion, I found an inexpensive chain with a small blue dolphin figure. I thought this would be appropriate for a teenage girl. Joop loved it, and we put it on right away. We were both happy. Of course, I was to find out later that in typical Joop fashion, she had conned me. Her birthday wasn't in July, it was in October. I had to laugh. Okay, her present was three months early. So what?

In the following months, Joop's condition deteriorated. More hospital visits and much lessened energy. When I asked Khun Usanee about Joop's deterioration, she explained that there were four stages to the AIDS process, each of increasing severity. Joop was now in the fourth and final stage. October came and Joop was now sixteen. An important age for any young girl. Sweet sixteen.

At the beginning of December, I learned that Joop was not doing well. She had been in the hospital for a spell and was now back at Mercy. The doctors said there was nothing more they could do for her. The Mercy staff should make her comfortable. Joop was in her final days. I planned to go visit her after work in the afternoon to comfort her. In the office, in the morning, I mentioned to Khun Usanee I would go to visit Joop that afternoon. Khun Usanee advised me not to go. She told me Joop had gone into hysterics when she was told she would not return to the hospital. Of course, she associated the stays at the hospital as providing care to keep her alive. She was desperate to live and screaming at the staff to take her to the hospital. Khun Usanee told me two of the nursing staff were with her and had given her some sedatives, but Joop was so agitated that the sedatives weren't taking effect.

Despite Khun Usanee's advice, after the lunch hour, I felt I had to go say goodbye. But it wasn't to be. As I walked into the open courtyard area, I could hear Joop screaming to go to the hospital. I hesitated but then started up the staircase leading to the third floor and the area of the AIDS ward where Joop was staying. When I got to the next landing, I stopped and listened. Joop was continuously screaming to go to the hospital. I wanted to see her, to hold her hand, but Joop associated me with the hospital visits. If she saw me, she would have hope she was to go to the hospital, that she was to live. My appearance would only make things much worse. I agonized over the decision but Khun Usanee was right. I turned and went home.

That was my last memory of Joop. At 3 p.m., Khun Usanee called me to let me know that Joop had just passed away. She assured me that the staff was washing the body and undertaking the necessary rituals to prepare her for a Buddhist funeral. It was so kind of Usanee to call. That was 3 p.m. of December 10, 2006. I always remember that time and date and Joop.

There were two more contacts with Joop. The next day Usanee gave me the chain with the small blue dolphin on it. Joop had been wearing it when she died and the staff knew I had given it to her. They gave it to Usanee to give back to me.

After a few days, we had the Buddhist cremation ceremony at Wat Saphan, it was called the Bridge Temple, as it was next to a bridge that passed over a nearby canal. This was where the kids from Mercy who passed away were cremated. The head monk was a very understanding and supportive man, and Fr. Joe and the staff respected him. Many of the staff were there as well as Fr. Joe, Sr. Maria, Khun Usanee and many of the senior Mercy kids. John MacTaggart and I were there from the volunteers who were at Mercy at the time. John was in tears, as was I, though I think I hid mine fairly well. The monks offered those attending the opportunity to go up and view Joop in the coffin before the cremation took place. All the kids present went up to see. I kept my seat.

One of the Soi 40 girls, Peung, turned back and asked me, "Khun Tom, don't you want to see?"

I told her I didn't want to see.

After the funeral ceremony, the head monk gathered the Mercy kids on the side and gave them a talk. I guess he was explaining how the cremation and funeral ceremonies fit into their religion. I thought it was a timely idea. A teaching moment, as they say, though a grim one. I didn't understand most of the talk, but one of the staff attempted to translate one point that I've never forgotten: *This life is an illusion.* I took it to mean that for a true Buddhist believer, it's important to remember that this life is just one in a cycle of lives. I believe what he meant is not to be attached to the things of this life, but to keep your eyes turned to the final enlightenment, after however many lives that takes. I decided I needed to learn much more about the tenets of Buddhism. I knew then what Fr. Joe meant when he said living with the Buddhists and the Muslims in the slum had made him a better Christian. Joop's spirit was now released to the next life and the path to enlightenment. I still keep contact with many of the Mercy kids I knew. Most of them are fully grown. At times, I wonder what mischief Joop would be doing now if she had been allowed to grow to adulthood. I miss you, Joop.

Galong at the Noodle Shop. Credit Mercy Centre

Galong and Fr. Joe.
Credit Mercy Centre

Sea Gypsy Girl and sister.
Credit Mercy Centre

Sea Gypsy village at Koh Lao. Credit Mercy Centre

Rail Line Kids, Fai and Khao. Credit Tom Crowley

Rail Line Kids, Khao Learning to Write. Credit Tom Crowley

Keng and U.S. Government Visitor. Credit National Archives

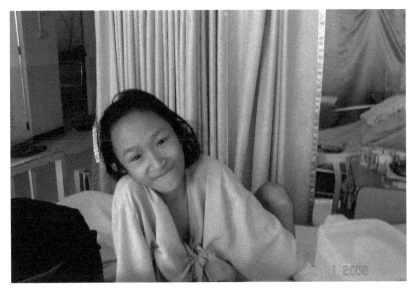

Joop Chang. Credit Tom Crowley

Chapter Nine

THE FLOOD — 2011

As a tropical country, Thailand receives heavy monsoon rains five to six months of the year at differing locations. Floods are also an annual event as the rivers bulge over their banks under the seasonal deluge of rain. Normally the floods are all kept somewhat under control, with just a few thousand farmers in the north of the country flooded out and their crops destroyed. In Bangkok it's not unusual for the heavy rains in September and October to overwhelm the storm drains and for the streets to flood with up to two feet of water or more on a weekly basis. This is normally not an issue for the Bangkok officials as the waters recede in a day or two. In such cases, it's business as usual in Thailand.

The year 2011 was a major exception. The rain fell in record-setting amounts, and flooding in the north of the country started as early as July. The government officials charged with letting water out of dams at catchment basins around the country during the early months of the season had not anticipated the flow. They had not prepared for the record rain and the dams overflowed. Parts of the country of commercial value, not only farms, were being flooded. The floodwaters continued to rise, and by October large areas of Bangkok and the sacrosanct financial districts were threatened.

The main river running through the center of Bangkok, the Chao Phraya, flowed down from the northern farm country. As the rain continued to fall, those responsible for managing the river at differing times and locations made the decision to drain as much as possible of the water breaching the banks into the rice fields along the river's course. The goal was to protect Bangkok at all costs. Of course, the diversion and resultant flooding destroyed the crops and the incomes of thousands of farm families.

The diversion efforts failed. The flooding was said to be the worst in fifty years, with one-third of the country flooded. In October, day by day, block by block, the city streets of northern and central Bangkok flooded, leaving standing water of three feet or more in places. It was a chaotic scene. The politicians in charge would warn people one day, "The flood is coming, run," and the next day, "All will be well, stay where you are." Of course, only one of those directives could be correct.

Unfortunately, the flooding continued and grew to overwhelm increasingly larger portions of Bangkok. Neighborhoods a bit away from the river were building levees to deter the water from those neighborhoods nearer the river. The result of the levees was that neighborhoods nearer the river retained higher levels of water rather than having it flow further into the city. Then fights started between the neighborhoods, with one group tearing down levees and another group building them back up to protect their homes. People were walking through knee- or waist-deep water or even boating through their neighborhoods.

A bit of comic opera was added when the owners of a crocodile farm near Bangkok announced that the farm had flooded and that over 300 crocodiles had escaped. A high official in the Parks and Wildlife Department told people not to be concerned and gave advice on how to handle the situation. "Hold a large palm leaf in each hand and, as you walk through the water, keep splashing down the leaves. This will frighten the crocodiles away." I suspect few people implemented this plan.

Despite such anecdotes, it was not an entertaining situation. There had been dark tales for years of Bangkok, with an elevation of just 4.9 feet, settling and slipping under the ocean waves. The population was in mortal fear. It wasn't just cloudy skies that darkened the city. The emotional impact was overwhelming for many. It seemed the apocalypse had arrived.

Ironically, the Mercy Centre itself, one hundred meters away from the Chao Phraya River but on the south side of Bangkok, was not inundated. The streets adjacent to Mercy, though, would be flooded twice a day with water of about two feet in depth, for an hour or so, when the two high tides came in.

Unlike the tsunami, this time there was no questioning, no meeting of the entire Mercy staff necessary to decide what to do. It was understood. Mercy must respond and help in its areas of responsibility. One of Fr. Joe's strengths was that he readily responded to emergencies. Indeed, one might think that he was, at some level, restored when an emergency, a fire, a flood, whatever, found Mercy.

The issue for Mercy was how to protect the preschools in flooded slum areas and the children and the families of those in our schools. Of the twenty-five Mercy preschools in operation at that time, our concern, as reported by Fr. Joe to supporters abroad, was for eleven schools in flooded areas. This involved over 800 preschool students, their families, and their teachers, totaling up to over 2,000 people.

As many as five or six of the schools were in areas where boats were needed to move through the neighborhoods. In addition, there were six other schools impacted in terms of access but not completely underwater. The school floor might or might not be dry, and going to and from the schools was difficult for the teachers, the children, and their families, but the schools continued to be open. Hundreds of thousands of people in Bangkok were isolated, short of food, and in danger of disease. The Thai army was working in many areas to evacuate people at risk and secure them in camps with food and medicine until they could return home. At Mercy, it was decided that our job was to maintain the schools in the flooded areas, provide food for the daily lunches, get more food for the family if needed, provide medicine, offer emergency transportation, and all the while keep the schools open.

This was in no way as significant as the tsunami work Mercy had undertaken previously, but still a remarkable step up for a Bangkok street charity to take. So that I would understand the effort that Mercy was making for those our schools served, Fr. Joe invited me to go along on one of the runs out to a school in a flooded area.

Choi, the Mercy staffer who had filled a key role in the tsunami work, had been appointed by Fr. Joe to lead the way. We met with him in the morning in front of Mercy so that he could guide us out to the school. I knew immediately that this would be a major project as the double-cab pickup truck he was driving was a high rider. It was a large truck with very large wheels. My guess was that the bottom clearance of the truck was close to three feet.

We drove north toward the flooded areas of Bangkok and kept going after arriving at the water's edge on a city street about five miles away from Mercy. As we drove along the increasingly flooded streets, the only vehicles we saw were similar in proportion to our truck, pushing small waves ahead of them as they moved slowly along. I thought the truck would carry us all the way, but it couldn't. We came to a side street, a turnoff toward the school, and pulled up in three feet of water at the intersection. There was a small recreational style fishing boat with planks for seats and an outboard motor parked there waiting for us. We carefully clamored down from the truck into the boat. The water was too deep down the side street for the truck to go forward. It would wait for us at the intersection with the main street.

As I looked down the side street, there were no vehicles, rather only one or two small boats with outboard motors much like ours. It was an urban setting with older townhouses crowded side by side. In Bangkok, it would be considered a middle-class neighborhood. Some people who had refused to leave their homes were standing here and there on house porches.

As we went along, one of the boats coming toward us stopped to pick up a couple of people from a house. It was serving as a water taxi. These people had decided not to leave their home for fear of looters who had been spotted going into houses in flood-abandoned neighborhoods. The water taxi would take them out to an area where they could buy food and water and then bring them back so they could guard their home. I can't remember what fees the taxis charged, but I understood they were expensive. The water taxis were impromptu commercial vehicles, responding to a profit opportunity. They were not there to assist poor families.

It was a clear day, no rain. Bangkok in October is still extremely hot, and the temperature was above ninety degrees Fahrenheit. A boat ride might have been nice except for the scene of abandoned homes in the muddy, refuse-stained floodwaters. We wove in and out among the town shops of the side streets, with the neighborhoods visibly poorer in appearance with each succeeding block, until we finally approached an area surrounded by a chain link fence. The boat nosed slowly into a driveway leading up four feet to a concrete pad that held a small hall and next to it a one-story wooden building. This was the Mercy preschool, being used as a temporary aid shelter. The teachers and children were on hand, and they were cooking lunch. Besides the children, some of the families who lived nearby were gathered on the dry ground in the hall beside the school. It was an island setting that would be safe as long as the water didn't rise further. Our supplies of food and water would go both to the staff and kids of the school and to the families from the neighborhood. We had a nurse with a medical kit along who looked after those who needed care.

Thai and World Bank sources dated October 2011, reporting on the flood in Thailand, cited up to 680 deaths, with an estimated 9.5 million people in 66 provinces affected. Don Muang, one of the two airports serving Bangkok, was flooded and closed for weeks. Several major industrial estates were flooded and the factories closed.

After a few weeks, the water started to recede, but in that time, Mercy had provided a lifeline to the children, their families, the teachers in our preschool program, and all those we met along the way who needed help. This mission, much like the tsunami relief program, demonstrated to me once again that within Mercy's fiber there is the essence of community care and responsiveness that came to light especially in times of emergency. I had the responsibility of reporting to our donors. In responding, Mercy had incurred significant costs above our normal operating costs. While the number of our twenty-five preschools and families affected was limited to a few thousand, not the tens of thousands of victims of the tsunami, the principle for Mercy remained the same. Mercy responded when the poorest of families were in need.

Gee, from Jail to Wedding

Gee was one of the many boys Kuhn Samran rescued from juvenile jail. This was around 2006. I believe Gee was sixteen or seventeen at the time. Gee's detention in the juvenile jail facility was due to the possession, not selling, of drugs. It was not uncommon for the drug dealers in Jet Sip Rai to coerce teens into running the drugs to customers. Unfortunately, the cops often caught the kids, not the dealers. That was Gee's case. Usually, at that time in the slum area near the port, the drugs for sale were amphetamines, which the long-haul truck drivers would look to buy when they came to the nearby port facility to pick up their loads.

Gee was a typical poor boy in many respects. He was short, skinny, a bit unkempt at all times, and never an A student. His parents were gone, though the cause was unknown, and he had been left to the abusive care of an uncle. To say he lacked confidence would be an understatement. His appeal lay in his constant striving, and he had an interest in music. Mary McLean's ad hoc music program for the Mercy kids helped Gee get a guitar and develop his technique.

His big interest during his time at Mercy was in the band that the boys formed. One weekend, probably on a Sunday, I wandered over to the girls' house on Soi 40. As I was approaching, I saw that the big sliding doors to what had been the loading side of the warehouse that now comprised the home were open.

As I entered, I was hit with a blast of music. It was a Credence Clearwater Revival song. CCR had been one of my favorite bands in my much younger days and the song was a classic rock song, "Have You Ever Seen the Rain." *Whoa, Mercy, what are you doing today?*

As I walked in, I found myself just off stage behind those watching the band's practice session. A group of the Soi 40 girls were gathered around watching the session and loving the music. I joined them. The band was struggling a bit, but what a great song for a bunch of teenagers in Bangkok to be struggling with. I learned from Mary the band also played a lot of the Cranberries and some Thai rock tunes. They called the band the Baby Ghosts. God knows why.

The interesting thing for me was that the atmosphere at the practice session was like something from my high school days. Remember the "in-crowd" you wanted to be part of in high school? Slum kids never get to be part of the in-crowd in any school. They're lucky just to be in school. However, as I watched the kids tuned into the band for those few moments, I could tell the Soi 40 kids felt as if they were the in-crowd. How cool was it having our own rock band? The Baby Ghosts became a sensation, if a brief one, in the Jet Sip Rai slum. Gee was one of the guitarists, and I think having that opportunity, while not leading to a career in music, did a lot for his self-confidence. He drew a picture of the band and gave it to Mary. She described it as "all hair and attitude."

Sometime after embarking on the rock music trail, Gee entered the Buddhist monkhood for three weeks. This is something Mercy encourages. It's a common ritual and rite of passage for teenage boys in Thailand. The rituals, the time spent in meditation, and the disciplined life at the temple were a great experience and helped to build Gee's belief in himself. He was proud of his time as a monk. At one point he was allowed to visit Mercy in his orange robes, completely shaven (no eyebrows), showing a composure that was new for him.

Gee soon reached eighteen, the age at which kids would leave Mercy to go out on their own. We lost track of him for a while. There was a fear that he had gone back to running drugs to make his money. Then I heard from Khun Samran that he was working at a street vendor's stand selling fried chicken at night. These stands, pushed along on bicycle-like wheels, were a hallmark of Bangkok and could be found all throughout the city on busy street corners twice a day, during the morning rush to work and during the evening return trip. They offered quick hot meals to the pedestrians of chicken, fish, corn, tom yum gung (spicy shrimp soup), congee (the popular Chinese rice porridge), and more. The stand Gee was working at was on the sidewalk near a red-light area that had good foot traffic, though it was competing side by side with other food stands. The hours these stands were open, depending on the vendor's stamina, were from roughly 7 p.m. to 2 a.m. when the bars closed.

I was worried about Gee's night working situation and decided to go take a look. When I got there, I stood back to watch, and there was no doubt that Gee was working hard. The stand was busy, there was constant movement, there was a line, and the fried chicken was flying to the customers. It looked like a moneymaking situation. Gee was working hard and was, of course, an assistant. The person in charge was a Thai lady in her thirties. She projected strength and decisiveness. The stand was orderly in operation and Gee was well directed. I left feeling pretty good about it. Gee was working hard but it was good, honest work. As long as he stuck to it, he would be okay.

A couple of months later, Khun Samran came to let me know the really good news. Gee was getting married. It was the lady who ran the chicken cart business Gee was working at. I didn't attend the wedding on a Friday morning, all was being organized by the bride, but Samran told me that the newlyweds would be coming over to Mercy about midday, after the wedding, to get Fr. Joe's blessing as Gee's acting father.

I was able to get there in time. Gee and the bride were standing at the entranceway to the Mercy courtyard and Fr. Joe, Khun Samran, and several of the staff were on hand. It was well worth the effort to be there. The lady was dressed in a brand-new pink dress. Gee was dressed all in white, wearing a white suit, which, no doubt, the bride had purchased. I called it the Jackie Chan look. At first, I almost couldn't recognize him. As they say, he cleaned up well. Never had he looked so good. There was no doubt he was living clean as his bride was apparently limiting the number of cigarettes he could smoke each day. He was a proud and beaming groom throughout our meeting and Fr. Joe's blessing. The bride was wearing her wedding gift, a gold chain. I presumed that in the way of the poor, she had brought it for Gee to give to her. It would be portrayed to her family as his wedding gift. That was important.

They had a small entourage with them. Khun Samran told me that in the afternoon they would be taking a train ride up to the northeast of Thailand, Ubon Ratchathani on the border with Laos and Cambodia. This was the farm community into which the bride had been born. After meeting the bride's family and staying over a few days, they would be returning to their chicken vendor business in Bangkok.

It was a glorious occasion, and the wedding was, I hope, Gee's salvation. He certainly would be well directed in life.

Credit to Mary McLean.

Vietnam—April 1967—Friendly Fire

My desire to get back into combat to redeem myself was soon blunted by army reality. On my return to my unit in Cu Chi, I asked the battalion commander to let me take up my platoon leader position once again. He refused my request for what I thought was a rather perverse reason. He was very happy with my performance and thought I should make the military my career. To boost me along that path, he told me I was to be assigned to what is termed the operations section of the battalion, where the plans were made for the troop movements in the field. I had no choice, so I flew out to join the battalion operations group in the field.

After spending a month down near the Mekong delta, the division received orders to change our focus. We were to move toward the north in the area closer to the Cambodian border.

We were to set up a camp for the battalion headquarters, and the rifle companies would operate deeper into the forest to intercept VC supply routes. This area had seen active fighting the previous year. The general feeling in the battalion was that this was "Indian country," as we said in Vietnam about areas considered to have a strong enemy presence. We would be seeing action for sure.

The entire battalion headquarters and support groups were transported by trucks in a major convoy. Our goal was to link up at the end of the day with one of the rifle companies and set up a perimeter within the woods. I was still of the mind that I wanted Charlie to come after us so I could play some active combat role. So I was happy to be on the move and happy at the prospect of entering an area important to Charlie.

As we rode along on a broken asphalt road there were no real villages, just clusters of homes along the road here and there. Then we branched off onto an increasingly narrow dirt road leading into the forest. There were no incidents along the way, and I hadn't expected any.

We left the trucks in mid-afternoon and moved by foot several kilometers further into the woods to an area where Paul Bunyan, the giant Minnesota woodsman, had apparently been let loose to swing his ax. Everywhere there were large craters and entire uprooted trees lying in a sideways forest it was almost impossible to walk through. This had been the site of a B-52 bomb strike sometime in the previous month or so. There must have been some intelligence of a large VC or NVA unit moving through the area, and in the absence of infantry units to engage them directly, division headquarters must have called for an Arc Light, the code name given to a B-52 tactical strike. These planes had most probably flown from U-Tapao airbase in Thailand, just over an hour's flight away.

For the most part, we were happy to use the site of the bombing as a night position. The craters provided readymade foxholes for many of the battalion. Those who weren't in the craters could dig in, as I did, in what was called a two-by-two-by-you. We would dig a hole two feet deep, two feet wide, long enough to fit our height, and pile the dirt in an embankment to catch bullets or shrapnel. When we were on the move and not in contact, this type of hole was considered adequate.

As dark fell, the rifle company sent out two squads (ten men each) a kilometer out in differing directions as ambush patrols. Two listening posts with two soldiers each were also put out just a hundred meters from the perimeter. The ground was dry, as the rainy season had not really started yet, and I was ready for a quiet night, not expecting Charlie to react to our presence so quickly.

It started about 10 p.m., with a sharp whistling sound I had never heard before, and then a tremendous cracking explosion causing the earth to shake beneath me. I had been asleep off and on, thinking it was going to be a long night, not really comfortable in my hole in the ground. The first explosion was followed by another and then another. I was as sorry as hell that I hadn't dug deeper. I hugged the bottom of my foxhole as closely as I could, grabbing at the dirt, trying to throw more of it out and get lower in any way possible.

Shells kept screaming in and exploding all around us. These weren't mortar shells. Mortar shells only made a soft coughing noise when they were fired and were virtually silent as they came in, with more of a "whump" sound when the rounds exploded. These explosions were much, much stronger. These were high-velocity artillery shells. The terrifying noise, the impact, and the fear they generated were tremendous. I couldn't think of anything except digging deeper, clawing through the earth, and praying for survival.

Then it stopped. The shelling hadn't lasted long in real time, only fifteen or twenty minutes or so, maybe a bit less. But for those of us on the ground, it was the longest twenty minutes of our lives. What the hell was it? I could hear that question asked repeatedly, along with cursing, yelling, and cries for a medic throughout the camp.

I was numb. I didn't move for a while. I just laid there. We weren't under direct attack, so there was nothing to be done. After a few minutes, I sat up, trying to hear better what was going on with the battalion command group sited in a crater only twenty meters from me. I was wondering what orders might be given. I heard the battalion CO on the radio reporting back to Brigade. He said we had been shelled and was demanding to know what the hell was going on. We had no reports of NVA artillery in the area, but this was definitely artillery fire. I had not been on the receiving end of artillery fire before, and the whole unit was in shock. I heard the report being made on the radio that we had two dead and several wounded. Evacuation of the wounded would have to wait until morning: there was no easily available space for a medevac chopper at night. A cleared area for the chopper to land would have to be blasted among the trees in the morning.

The rest of the night was quiet. In the morning I went over to the battalion command group and got a report. This was a case of what was called "friendly fire." The artillery fire had come from a Vietnamese

Army 105 mm artillery unit. They said they had not been informed of a U.S. army unit moving into the area. They were firing a routine pattern of harassment and interdiction (H&I) fire, as part of their plan to stop Charlie from moving through the area. This type of fire did not focus on observed targets. Rather, the artillery battery would just pick an area where intelligence stated that Charlie might be moving troops or supplies at night and fire some rounds into that area. It was a common and pretty much useless tactic in Vietnam.

What it normally meant was that one gun would be fired every ten seconds or so, rather than the whole battery of six 105-mm cannons at once. This was a lifesaver for us. If all six cannons had been firing at the same time over a sustained period, in what the artillery termed "fire for effect", the area would have been obliterated and our casualties would have been at least ten times the number we sustained. But that was small comfort to those of us on the ground.

Everyone in the unit was dumbfounded. Either our command had not clearly communicated our movement to our ARVN ally, resulting in our soldiers being killed, or as an increasingly popular theory had it, the ARVN unit was really on Charlie's side and had feigned misunderstanding of the situation to shell an American unit. The result of either belief was that our leadership was considered pretty stupid, and morale instantly sank very low.

Stories of the soldiers who had been killed circulated rapidly. One soldier was the radio telephone operator for the commanding officer of the infantry company securing the site where we had camped for the night. During the shelling, the CO had been on the radio handset, urgently asking the patrols if they could determine the direction of the incoming fire so we could radio for support to counter-fire. The RTO had been seated next to him holding the radio. A piece of shrapnel had flown between them, cutting the phone cord and the throat of the RTO. He had bled out quickly.

We stayed on that site one more night. It all contributed to the feeling that our military had tremendous power, but no idea how to direct it in a way that made any sense.

War is about killing. At the same time, if one is to cling to any sense of moral rightness, the killing has to be necessary. It had to involve defending yourself, your buddies, and implicitly the country that had put you in the field. The cumulative effect of my months in combat and seeing what we were doing in Vietnam was that I began to question the necessity of the war and our killing. It increasingly seemed a form of insanity. I am certain my feelings reflected those of many of the grunts I lived with, as they often approached me with the same doubts and questions about the validity of our participation in Vietnam. I had no ready answers.

Chapter Ten

THE MERCY SCHOOLS/ THE MERCY TEACHERS 1972-PRESENT

At the end of the day, the first-grade teacher Kru Tuk dismissed her kids and went around the classroom looking for whatever might have been left behind. She was surprised to find that one of the students, a nine-year-old girl, Malee, had stayed behind. Yes, she was nine years old and just in first grade. The girl, abandoned by her parents and living with an uncle, had been very delayed in starting her schooling as her uncle had felt it wasn't necessary. "Girls don't need to go to school."

Her teacher, Kru Tuk, was one of the few adults the girl trusted. Malee asked if she could sleep inside the teacher's house that night. She said she could sleep just inside the mosquito netting. She wouldn't be trouble. Kru Tuk asked the girl why she wanted to stay with her. The girl said nothing, she just looked away. The teacher understood. Malee was being abused at home. Kru Tuk called Mercy and said she had a young girl who needed protection. The Mercy staff told her not to hesitate, to bring the girl in right away.

There is much more to this story, told by Fr. Joe, but the bottom line is that by 3 a.m. the girl was safe at Mercy. Still, the uncle who had been molesting her made trouble. He lodged a complaint with the police, who then brought the guy to Mercy's front gate the next morning. The Mercy staff wouldn't allow them entry. The uncle was determined to confront the poor girl who was inside near an open second-floor balcony of the Mercy building overlooking the street. The uncle stood in front of the building and shouted to her. He ordered her to come home. He told her he loved her.

From inside Mercy, the girl shouted back, "You don't love me. You hurt me."

The police asked the Mercy staff to allow them to question the girl and the Mercy staff refused. The police officers were all men. The staff told them to come back with a female officer. There were no female officers at the slum station.

Later a female officer was found to interview Malee with Mercy staff present. The officer got the full story. Malee stayed with Mercy. When the case went to court, the judge, God bless him, sided with Malee and Mercy. Mercy became her home, and she was protected and went to school at Mercy. Over the years, thousands of poor children have been saved this way through the Mercy preschool system. The slum teachers, not just in the Mercy preschools, but in all of the government primary schools in the slums in which Mercy works, know the Mercy Home is there for children at risk. The teachers are often the first step toward protection for abused children.

In my first visit in the beginning days of my apprenticeship at Mercy, the Mercy Centre was a drab gray building, but it had one source of color: the kids. When I entered the courtyard, the kids, yelling and running, the splash of color from their bright white and blue uniforms, were a welcome sight to me. Two of the preschool classes took place directly across from the entrance and on the other side of a gravelly parking lot. Many of the schools then were semi-outdoor affairs. The kids studied while seated on benches under tin roofs with bamboo walls. There was only one wooden wall to the structure: the other wall areas were large openings for air circulation. The Mercy schools were the first program Joe had mentioned to me during our initial talk. The two-room wooden structures were not impressive. I was to learn that the very act of collecting the children, with some of the women from the slum teaching and watching over them during the day, was a breakthrough idea for the slum. It was daycare as well as education.

As it was in the beginning, so it continues today, the heart of Mercy consists of the preschool system. Moms, maybe a bit more educated now than in the beginning, possibly just poor moms now, not slum moms, are at the front line for Mercy, to contact the families, to promote education, and to promote the welfare of the children.

I have mentioned some of this before. I believe taking a deeper look into how the schools came into being and grew to become the heart of Mercy is necessary to an understanding of the unique impact of Mercy's programs.

Of course, it was Sr. Maria's years of work in the Jet Sip Rai slum area, and her knowledge of the family situations of the poor she had vowed to serve, that allowed the first contacts to be made. Mercy was, and is, very much a woman's organization in that the great majority of the staff are women. They make many of the daily decisions. It was Sr. Maria's woman-to-woman contact and the trust she had built up in Jet Sip Rai that underwrote the initiation of the Mercy preschool in the slaughterhouse district. The slum moms knew then and today that they can trust their mother figure, Sr. Maria.

The first school was started near the slaughterhouse in 1972. Further interest from community leaders in having a preschool in other areas of the slums came almost immediately. The number of schools and the number of children attending grew each year until, in the early 2000s, the number of Mercy preschools had grown to over thirty, and the total number of children in attendance had grown to as many as 2,000 at times. The schools have two levels: the entry level is the three and four-year-olds, and the second level is the five and six-year-old children. The subjects of study are the basic courses, math, reading, and writing, with a bit of music, song, dancing, and art along the way. Graduation ceremonies for the six-year-old children, in March at the end of the Thai school year, are a big deal. Today the kids wear caps and gowns, provided by Mercy. The families come to see their children graduate and they receive a diploma. It is a festive occasion with balloons floating and the families take pictures galore.

With each graduation group, Fr. Joe gives a talk to motivate the children and the families. The message is a simple and powerful one, stressing the importance of education. Go to school. If you are tired when you wake up, go to school. If you have no breakfast, go to school. If it's raining, go to school. This message is stressed by Fr. Joe to a community in which education has not been a hallmark. Poor kids would traditionally go to work as soon as they were able to earn a few baht of Thai currency. School was forgotten. Fr. Joe's talk was as much for the parents in attendance as for the children. Go to school. Education will see you through life.

It was a powerful innovation in that at that time in Thailand, the Thai public school system had no kindergarten or preschool program. The result was that when these slum kids finished the Mercy program at age six and moved into first grade in the government primary school system, they had, what the American school system calls a head start. The poorest of children would start off at the head of the class, not behind.

Mercy schools today can also be found in the construction camps that abound in Bangkok. The camp conditions and shacks are much worse than those in the slums, in that they often lack access to running water and electricity. While the parents work a ten-to-twelve-hour day constructing the Bangkok high-rise buildings, the children are left alone in shacks in a dirty, rubble-strewn lot. At one time, these day laborers came from Isan, the northeastern farm area of Thailand. Today most come from Burma or Cambodia. Assisting them has not been a priority for the Thai government.

On one occasion I was asked to go with teachers from the Mercy School department to visit one such camp, found by a Mercy outreach team on the outskirts of Bangkok. It was a fifty-minute drive through increasingly smaller streets and older buildings. We finally came to a large lot the size of a football field with a temporary wooden fence thrown up around it. On one side of the lot was a drainage ditch with about thirty wooden shacks lined up alongside it. We drove into the lot and parked. As the teachers got out of the car, a crowd of fifteen or twenty children and five or six adult women came out. This was the third trip by the team to evaluate how Mercy could place a school in the camp. The camp had been there for over a year. The contractors used it as a base for their workers, whom they would pick up in trucks in the morning and take back to the camp at night.

The children we visited that day were excited about our arrival and mobbed the teachers, burying them in questions. One girl, about eight or nine was crying and holding on to the hand of one of the teachers. I asked what the problem was. The teacher told me the girl was afraid that we wouldn't come back. She was desperate. She had never been taught to read or write in any language. She was old enough to understand that she was losing her chance at life, and she was afraid. It was a departure from the focus on preschool children, but with the help of Canadian architect Graeme Bristol and Ms. Cavelle Dove of the Canadian International Aid Agency (CIDA), Mercy was able to build and open a school in that lot to provide education through the sixth grade. The girl who was crying learned how to read and more.

What was not immediately obvious to me when I joined Mercy, but what I came to understand over time, is that the school system is at the core of Mercy's excellence as a social welfare organization. The teachers of the slum children are themselves from the slum. They are moms who love their children at home and the children they teach, with a deep understanding of the lives the children lead and their needs. The beginning of the Mercy Home program grew out of the teachers finding children in their classes who were being abused in some way. The teachers brought the abused children to the attention of Fr. Joe and Sr. Maria, stressing that these kids needed a refuge only Mercy could provide.

With the Mercy Home program, the connection that Mercy had in the slum areas deepened. Other children were brought into Mercy by adults who had become aware of Mercy through the teachers at the schools. As Mercy became known as a refuge for all abused children in the slums, it was natural that the staff would develop an awareness to look after the older children in need. The Mercy Street Kids Outreach program began and grew with the need it found in the slums.

I believe the combination of these three programs, the Mercy Schools, the Mercy Home, and the Mercy Street Kids Outreach program, have allowed Mercy to become what we in the business world call a "center of excellence." There are other children's homes throughout the world, but the linkage of the system of preschools at Mercy to its other programs has given it the unique opportunity to be aware of and to reach out to great numbers of children, and by extension, the many families in need in the Bangkok slums.

As an update during this time of Covid, with the schools closed for in-person teaching, many have been converted into community aid centers. Mercy teachers are on hand, camping at the schools overnight in sleeping bags and tents, to distribute food partially funded by the government. Without work, many in the slums are going hungry. Mercy schools are in the center of the areas needing relief. Mercy's cooperation with the government has made it easier for both to provide much-needed assistance to thousands of slum dwellers during the Covid lockdown.

The Mercy preschools were an innovative program in Thailand in 1972. They became the basis for the excellence that Mercy has achieved across the board since then. Kudos to Fr. Joe and Sr. Maria. In the appendix, there is a short list of the awards Mercy has received over the years.

Lumpini Park Mom and Her Two Kids

I was at times unsure whether to call on Mercy to take in kids I saw on the street. The issue is that they probably have parents somewhere on the scene. The law in Thailand is very clear on parental rights. The wife belongs to the husband. The kids belong to the parents. I was told by Mercy staff that they had limited power to intervene in family problems. They told me if a Thai cop was walking by a house in the Jet Sip Rai slum area and the husband was beating the wife, the cop would ignore it and just keep walking. I hope that may not be so much the case today, but I'm sure the principle remains.

We had a case in which a well-meaning foreigner reported to Mercy that a young girl, about ten years old and dressed very poorly, was begging on the streets late at night, 10 p.m. or so. She would sit on a crosswalk bridge over the Rama IV Road adjacent to the slum. There was a Tesco-Lotus supermarket mall on one side and a Big C supermarket mall on the opposite. There was plenty of foot traffic, even later at night, as both sides had fast food outlets. Two staff from the Mercy Street Kids Outreach program went to see the girl.

What they found was that her grandmother had put her out to beg. The girl was in school and satisfied to be with her grandmother. We thought she was at risk, and the Mercy staff was not happy with the situation, but the grandmother was well within the scope of her parental rights. This was the reality Mercy staff had to work with, and I had to also in any effort to help them.

Lumpini Park is a beautiful, shady, green oasis in the center of Bangkok, surrounded by very busy streets, with high-rise office towers and hotels overlooking the park. One very hot day, after a nearby lunch meeting with a donor, I decided to walk through the tree-shaded coolness of the park to look for a taxi at a street corner a block away. Leaving the park to return to the roadside, I saw a mom and two kids sitting outside on the sidewalk along the park fence. The road was the busy Thanon Witthayu (wireless road), awash with noxious carbon monoxide fumes exploding from the cars racing by. The mom and kids were very dirty and wearing ragged clothes. From the style of their dress, I guessed they were from the countryside. Probably, once again, a farm family had come to Bangkok looking for work and had stumbled down. It seemed to me that they had most likely spent the night sleeping rough inside the park. The park closed at 10 p.m., but any number of homeless people would hide in the bushes until the park police had passed by, and then settle down for the night. The mom was slumped down, looking toward the road, just staring. The kids were on either side of her, twisting around, hanging on to the park fence, but also looking lost.

I hesitated. Someone should talk with the mom and see if she needed help. However, if I went back to Mercy to find the counselors necessary to offer her help, it would take a while, possibly a couple of hours, and the mom and her kids might be gone by the time someone was able to come. The street scene in Bangkok was fluid, to say the least.

I wanted to help but decided I needed to have permission. I called Khun Usanee at Mercy and described the situation. "Would it be okay if I brought the family into Mercy?"

She said, "Yes, of course."

I went up to the mom and asked her if they were okay. She just shook her head no and looked away. I asked where they were staying. Could I help them to get home? Now she looked at me, but again she shook her head no.

Finally, I asked, "Are you hungry? Do you need to eat?"

Now she looked straight at me and nodded yes. I told her I worked at a home for kids and described Mercy. I asked her if they would come with me in a taxi and go to Mercy to get some food and help. She was apprehensive but nodded yes. Her kids were just watching as if it was the moon landing. I doubt if they had seen any foreigners in the countryside, much less their mother talking to one.

So we started. I had to hustle them across the busy street, dodging traffic, so we could catch a taxi going in the right direction. All the time I was talking to the mom, encouraging her to trust me. I doubt if she had ever taken a taxi ride, and I'm sure the streets of Bangkok were a hot, messy puzzle to her. The kids stayed close, now clinging to their mom, unsure of what was happening.

Once we were in the taxi, me in the front seat, the mom and her kids in the back seat, all visibly uncomfortable, I was able to relax a bit. Maybe this would work out. The issue now was the taxi driver. Drivers normally did not want to go to the Jet Sip Rai slum area where Mercy was. This guy, however, was a hero. After a brief uncertain glance at me, he listened to me talking to the mom and kids and signed on for the program. He didn't say a thing. I gave him the directions at each turn and talked to the mom, describing Mercy and assuring her she and the kids would be taken care of.

We arrived at the main Mercy building in about twenty minutes. Now I was thankful for the new buildings I had criticized some years before. These buildings would seem like normal office buildings on a business street in Bangkok. In the slum setting, they projected substance, important for people who had lost their footing in life. The taxi driver and the mom both looked at the imposing frontage of Mercy, and the welcoming signs in front, and relaxed. This place seemed okay.

After giving the taxi driver a nice tip, I guided the mom and kids up the front steps into the Mercy courtyard. Khun Usanee had alerted one of the staff ladies who was waiting for us. She went straight to the family, saying she would take care of them. I told the mom I had to go to work, but that they would be okay now. Again, she said nothing but just nodded her head to me. She was still somewhat uncertain, I thought.

A few hours later, I went back to the courtyard prior to going home. The family was sitting there, all cleaned up, in new clothes, well-fed, and smiling, though I felt that they were still somewhat uncertain. Why not? Their world was moving quickly. I spoke to the staff lady working with them, and she said that the mom wanted to go home to their farming village and relatives in the north. They would stay at Mercy overnight. The next day a Mercy staffer would get them tickets, give the mom some pocket money, and put them on the bus home.

I said goodbye and went on home, feeling that on that day, I had done some good at Mercy. It was a great feeling. Mercy made it possible.

There are inevitable failures when working with the neediest of children and families. Those failures hurt badly, but what Fr. Joe had told me once was very true. You must consign the failures to the burden the angels could carry and let go of the guilt. Also, you must celebrate the successes you achieve. This event was one occasion for me to celebrate. It was a good day.

Vietnam—September 1967—
Riding Home with the Guys

The day that all overseas troops wait for, the day that every soldier serving in Vietnam planned for immediately upon arrival in country, finally arrived. The military term is DEROS. Without the military doubletalk, DEROS means it's time to go home, to go back to the world as we would say. Every serviceman or servicewoman in Vietnam would keep a calendar marked with how many days were left before they would be going home. It wasn't significant in the beginning. I mean, three hundred days to go, two hundred days to go, that was a time frame you couldn't really feel. However, once you got down to a hundred days to go, that became a magic number. Then you were becoming a short-timer. That term, *short-timer*, often signaled to others, especially your commanding officers, that you shouldn't be put in a danger zone, *I'm going home soon.* The short-timer's calendar was a special calendar and every trooper you spoke to knew where they stood on it. The common phrase they would recite when asked was, ninety days and a wake-up, or fifty days and a wake-up. I never spoke with any short-timer who didn't know exactly how much time they had left. On my second-to-final day, I was called back from the field to the Cu Chi base camp and given my travel orders home.

Hitching a ride on military transport is one of the advantages of military life, but it can be a double-edged sword. It is a very ad hoc system, and you can't know what inconvenience awaits you along the way. I was on my way back to the States and would ordinarily have been given a voucher for a seat on a civilian plane under contract to the military. However, at my request, I had been granted what was called a delay in route to my new military assignment in the U.S. This provided me with written orders giving me permission to stop in Japan and take leave on my way back. That meant I had to hitch rides on any military cargo planes going my way. As we had an ongoing war in the Pacific area, there was no problem getting rides. There was a tremendous two-way flow of military air traffic from the U.S. to Vietnam and other points in the Pacific.

The first leg of my trip was to be from Tan Son Nhut Air Base in Saigon to Yokota Air Base just outside of Tokyo. This was an easy ride to catch as all planes going back to the U.S. had to stop in Yokota to refuel. I had caught a chopper down to Tan Son Nhut and spent the night in a transient officers' hooch at Camp Alpha, the place I had originally checked into on arrival in Vietnam a year before. The next morning, I changed uniforms from my jungle fatigues to the short-sleeved khakis the army considered Class A dress for the tropics and, in summertime, northern hemisphere wear. This was mandatory during that period for any soldier traveling on military orders. The idea was to present the best possible image of the U.S. military to the public while traveling through the U.S. and around the world. Somewhere along the line, possibly after the first Gulf War, some bright PR lights in the Pentagon evidently changed the thinking, believing that if the military went through transportation points in the U.S. in their utility uniforms, then the public would have the fact of war rubbed in their faces and be more inclined to support the war effort.

I was very put out that morning. I'd had a pretty sleepless night, given the excitement and emotion of leaving Vietnam for good and being able to look forward to civilian comforts. In addition, the dispatch office for soldiers seeking military rides, where I had to report in, show my orders, and wait for a flight going my way that had room for me, was not far from a Quonset building that emitted some strong and disagreeable odors. I asked around and learned that this was the Tan Son Nhut mortuary. This was one of the mortuaries where they received the bodies of soldiers killed in action and prepared them for the trip back home to be buried. Whether the odors consisted of the chemicals used to prep the bodies or just the smell of decomposition that could come so quickly in the tropics, I wasn't sure. But the knowledge of the building's function, combined with the odors, worked badly on my mind.

I was very relieved when the officer handling the bookings called out my name and pointed out an Air Force cargo jet on the ramp, saying that I could ride out and get on that one. It was clearing to Yokota Air Base, and I was to be the only passenger.

However, when I climbed up the tail ramp to get on the plane, I discovered I was not to ride alone. There were six metallic-gray military caskets on board. They had been loaded two caskets side by side in a row and fastened down the center aisle of the plane. The crew chief pointed me toward the front and told me I would be alone on the flight, but of course, I wouldn't. I would be strapped in on a lateral bench seat alongside the front two caskets. These guys were my company, and I was theirs, on their last ride home. The crew chief left me and went forward to his flight station, out of my sight. I was left alone with the caskets.

I am sure the long plane ride home is one of serious introspection for all combat veterans. That would have been the case for me even without the company of these six soldiers. However, with the caskets in front of me as a focal point, my soul-searching was an extended, strong, and searing experience.

At least twice during the flight, I got up and walked around the row of caskets. I put my hands on each casket, paused while I thought about the young man inside and his family, and prayed for each one. I called up the memories of all my friends who had been killed and included them in my thoughts and prayers.

I don't know what a psychologist would say about enclosing a recent combat veteran with these caskets for such an extended period, but it was hardly a healing experience. Instead, I felt an anger growing inside of me and eventually focused my thoughts on that. I was angry at the loss. Not just the loss of the lives of these men or of my many friends, but angry at the loss of an innocence that could never be recovered. My soul had been scarred and altered and could never be restored. Just like Humpty Dumpty, I realized that some things, very important things emotionally, could never be put together again.

As I sat alone in that cold plane, looking at the caskets, I grew to understand the depth of emotional damage I and all combat veterans sustained. So many jumbled feelings went through my mind. It wasn't just the emotional damage and sense of loss that was the source of my growing anger. Rather it was my sense of loss combined with the knowledge that had been growing within me almost from my first days in Vietnam, that our leadership, political and military, had failed us in so many ways.

Myself, my buddies in combat, my brothers in the caskets I was riding along with, we had all grown to adulthood in a period of great faith in our government's political leadership on foreign policy issues, as well as faith that our military power was used to defend the country from foreign threat. We were the children of World War II and had judged the war in Vietnam in that light. Of course, there was no comparison between the threats to America involved in the two wars. The Japanese had directly attacked the U.S. at Pearl Harbor. Germany had declared war on the U.S. several days later.

In Vietnam, apart from a debatable domino theory, there was no real threat to America. That knowledge, built up through daily observation for a year, gave birth to a strong feeling of betrayal. We had been used. We had been used as tools of a bankrupt foreign policy by the politicians, and as cannon fodder for career military officers to advance in their race toward a star or two on their shoulders. So it was not just a loss of innocence; it was a loss of faith in our leadership and our cause. I was to learn that I wasn't alone. Hundreds of thousands of my combat brothers as well as millions of Americans at home would share that loss of faith.

I have had the chance to talk with Iraqi and Afghanistan War veterans in recent years, and one of the saddest things for me has been the repetition of those same thoughts and feelings fifty years later. As one of the guys in my platoon said to me many years later, "The army trained us for war. They didn't train us to come home." That is the same today. Many of the present-day vets feel used and come away with anger. We, the American people, never seem to learn; we perpetuate the cycle of faith in leaders, both political and military, who don't deserve our trust.

I have never forgotten riding home with the guys on that flight. Maybe that's what we need to have our political and military leaders do in each war, ride along back from the combat zone with the bodies of the men they ordered into battle. Especially those politicians who ran from military service. Forcing them to confront the reality of their leadership choices might make them reflect and consider those choices more carefully.

At that time, I had no understanding of what later came to be called post-traumatic stress disorder (PTSD). There were words used after World War I and World War II, such as *battle fatigue* or *shell shock,* to describe the strong emotional issues confronting combat veterans. I believe the public at that time saw it as a weakness on the part of the soldier, something not to be discussed, but rather to be covered up. However, possibly due to the large numbers of Vietnam veterans or the passing of time to the Iraq and Afghanistan wars, PTSD is now a recognized reality. It is a label given not just to veterans but to all those who suffer trauma: those who have been abused in family or social situations, those firefighters, police officers, and others who combat the destruction that visits our society. It is real. It can lead to substance abuse, depression, and suicides and in many other ways torment the victims throughout their lives. Over the following years, I was slowly to come to understand that I was carrying that burden. I was an angry man and acted out publicly and privately in damaging ways for myself and others, for which I apologize. Years later, at Mercy, I was to find a treatment for PTSD.

Chapter Eleven

LITTLE BIRDS —
2010-PRESENT

Three of the Little Birds girls died this past year. The terrible thing is that in a way, they made the decisions that led to their deaths. Starting life with the tremendous health burden of being HIV-positive, their medical decisions were always made for them. That is, those decisions were made for them if they were among those lucky children who were at Mercy. Those children in the slum community with no source of medicines or medical supervision simply had no future. But there came a time of independence, possibly the mid-teens or early twenties, when becoming young adults, the HIV-positive children chose to make medical decisions for themselves and to ignore some of the strict guidelines. Without conscious intent, they chose death.

The Little Birds group is a program developed by Mercy AIDS staff in recent years to help those youngsters transitioning into adulthood and community life make the right health decisions. Little Birds was formed separately from Mercy by volunteer staff from Mercy. The focus is on helping the HIV-positive children of Mercy to move into the adult world and society as they graduate from school. The major challenge they confront is the transition from the dependent institutional life and guidance of Mercy into independent roles in adult society.

Mercy's policy, to have the kids move on when they are eighteen and have finished their schooling, was understandable. We were always taking in younger children who were very needy. I had at one time talked with Fr. Joe about the possibility of Mercy setting up a halfway house in the city to help our graduates master the transition to adult life in a group setting. He was clear that he felt that was a step Mercy couldn't undertake. I didn't question him further, but I believe he thought we should keep our focus on the youngest of those children who came to Mercy. So be it. Our kids came from hard backgrounds, but we trusted that given a boost from Mercy, they would be able to confront the issues of going into society.

However, the HIV/AIDS kids were a special group of children within Mercy who have unique problems upon their departure from Mercy. That caused some concern and thought for Khun Usanee and the medical staff working with her. The HIV-positive children were, as the saying goes, very much special needs children. Within the organized setting of Mercy, they had friends and support. They would eat well, get plenty of rest, and would take their meds on the rigid schedule that was necessary. However, by 2010, it had become clear that some of the older kids, those who had gone into the adult work community, were not sticking to the schedule for the medicines or, in a few cases, not taking their meds at all. This came to light when we received calls that some of them, now in their late teens, were in the hospital, ill with AIDS-related symptoms. For AIDS patients, this is a disaster. When you have these setbacks, you can get on the medical regimen again and recover to some extent, but you have been set back permanently in your health, and in your body's ability to fight against the illnesses life can afflict on you. You must in the future continue to take the meds and take them on the rigid schedule required.

The growing number of Mercy kids in the "AIDS brigade" were our focus. I remember traveling to Toronto in 2006 to attend the World AIDS conference with Fr. Joe, Khun Usanee, and several of the aids staff. During the event, Usanee and I were standing together on the conference floor, which was filled with exhibits. As we looked around, there were stands for medical suppliers, various government AIDS assistance organizations, and representatives of various AIDS communities.

Khun Usanee asked me, "Khun Tom, do you know what is missing?"

I looked around and then answered no. Shaking her head in dismay, she waved her hand over the conference floor, "There is nothing here concerning children born HIV-positive."

I believe that is where she conceived her thought to establish Little Birds to help those departing from Mercy to adjust to life in the adult world.

Khun Usanee and the Mercy medical staff, all working as volunteers, decided to set up a program apart from Mercy to offer counseling and support in a group setting for those Mercy HIV/AIDS young adults now struggling with work and social life in the adult community. The program was open to younger HIV-positive Mercy kids, down to age twelve at times, on the basis they needed to learn the facts of living with AIDS also. I was happy when I was extended the chance to assist the project. The medical staff had all the contact information necessary to organize meetings with the group members to discuss their varying situations and needs. In the beginning, the medical team would hold discussions and feed the group lunch at the same time, as part of the teaching session. If their health needs wouldn't motivate them to come in for counseling sessions, the offer of a good group meal and chat would.

In December 2010, the volunteer Tew Bunnag was able to convince the Ramada hotel in downtown Bangkok to provide some meeting rooms for a day of instruction and group therapy with a buffet lunch included. It was a grand initiation for these teens and young adults in the form of group support that they needed so much. It convinced them we were serious. I have never seen a buffet disappear as completely as the seafood buffet the hotel set up that day.

Midway through the day, it struck me that it was a special date. It was four years to the day that Joop had passed away. If she had lived, she would have been part of this group. I mentioned it to Khun Usanee, but she gave me a patient look and just shook her head. It caused me to pause for a second, but then I understood. As a medical professional tending to AIDS patients, she had seen so many, many die. The past is the past. She didn't forget, but as a medical professional, had learned not to dwell on those memories. I wasn't a professional. I only had limited experience, and I couldn't let Joop go.

Thus was born the Little Birds group. It would go on to win awards from the Thai government for its innovative approach to assisting children born HIV-positive. The group would grow from forty HIV-positive members to 106 today. In a later stage, Little Birds would connect with another independent group, for those HIV-positive children going into adult life formed by a nurse from the Thai Red Cross. That combined group went on to link up with and assist groups of HIV-positive young adults organizing in over eight cities and towns in Thailand.

The medical counselors formed the routine of holding group

counseling sessions every month when possible. What was the counseling and assistance provided?

First on the agenda, at every meeting from the beginning, the counselors would emphasize to the Little Birds the absolute need to take meds, every day, on schedule. It may seem obvious and easy to do, but you must understand: outside of the support group, the Little Birds didn't want the rest of the world to know they were HIV-positive. They wanted to be "normal," whatever that meant in their differing settings. At work, in a busy setting, they didn't want to take time out to take their meds and have to explain to the others in the workplace what they were doing and why. If they were dating, they didn't want to let the other person know they were HIV-positive until they felt it was absolutely necessary.

There was one case where a bright, capable girl in the program didn't tell her boyfriend about her illness and became pregnant. The baby was delivered successfully. One of our Little Bird nurses was at the hospital with the boyfriend during the birth. He was a proud father. Only then did he learn from our nurse that the woman he loved was HIV-positive. He was, as we say in the U.S., "a stand-up guy." He didn't pause to say that it was okay, that he loved her, and they would manage things together. The only problem he was concerned about was how to tell his parents.

There is a happy ending. The boy's parents did accept the girl and their new grandson. I saw the couple together several times after that at Little Bird meetings and he was very much the devoted and supportive husband and father. The mother is strong and has become a leader within the Little Birds group. The baby is free of the virus, which can well be the case when an HIV-positive mother who takes the medications gives birth. He is healthy and growing big.

In addition to counseling on how to handle the stigma and discrimination being HIV-positive brings up in society, the other issues the group addresses in meetings are the everyday issues of teens going into society: how to find a job, how to manage the little money they may be making, and how to handle social and dating situations.

An important theme in all the meetings is counseling the kids on the need not to stigmatize themselves. They are innocent. They were born HIV-positive. A surprising problem is that even the medical world treating them can be insensitive to their struggle. The Little Birds get their medicine from the Thai government at a government hospital. One boy told the story of sitting in a waiting room to see the doctor and having the nurse come out and ask, in a loud voice, "Who's the AIDS patient?" The boy was humiliated. Thus, one goal of the Little Birds group came to be the education of the Thai medical community in an attempt to influence them to be more attuned to the patient's privacy.

One of the issues Khun Usanee and the staff encountered with the Little Birds group that became apparent after some time was that they were not taking responsibility for their actions and the group's direction. Rather, they waited until the staff said they should do something. They all came from a background at Mercy, where decisions were made for them. Mercy, as good as its heart may be, is an institution. The Little Birds had no experience of forming their own life. They were, in fact, institutionalized. We found they were waiting for decisions to be made for them and not really taking ownership of those decisions.

Usanee and the medical staff realized they had to take steps to turn the management of the group over to the teens and young adults. It was necessary to make them understand they were responsible for the decisions that would form their future. The first step toward that understanding was to make them responsible for the decisions made by the group. Elections were organized, and the group picked from itself the leaders who would lead the discussions and the decision-making process.

It was, to be sure, a slow process, but over time, at each monthly meeting, as the staff hung back, the kids started debating and making their own group decisions. Today, Little Birds has an active management team comprised of the group's members. The young leaders are respected within the group and within the Thai medical community.

One of the first group decisions was to be the name. *What do we want to be known as?* They came up with the name Little Birds, and that name has become known and respected by the other HIV/AIDS groups throughout Thailand.

It took several years of lobbying, but the Little Birds formed a foundation now officially recognized by the Thai Ministry of Health. The young Little Birds leaders and representatives take part in the annual national health review meetings of the Ministry. Patient advocacy for those in Thailand who are HIV-positive is now on the Ministry's discussion list. Little Birds staff and young leaders are now active in the World AIDS conference, representing the needs of HIV-positive children. These are all incredible accomplishments for what started as a self-help group for Mercy's HIV-positive kids

Sadly, as I wrote previously, this past year three of the Little Birds girls died. The societal pressures on the Little Birds members are enormous. At times, as one of the nurses told me, "They get sick of being sick and give up." They stop taking the medications, become progressively sicker, and, in time, die. It is an ongoing battle of counseling and education. As I write this, the volunteer medical staff, under Khun Usannee's direction, continue to work with the Little Birds group, helping them to cope with the current threat of Covid-19, manage themselves, and make the transition to adult life.

Mercy Kids Football

Mercy has had limited plans for what we might call special programs for the kids. Normally their activities revolved around school, meals, study, the art program a number of kids participated in on an ad hoc basis, a general play period each day, and football, which the boys love.

Girls can love football too, but I was to find that their participation was discouraged by some of the more conservative administrative staff. We once had an invitation, from the British coach of the Thai national team, for Mercy to bring a group of kids out to see the team practice. As you can imagine all these football-crazy slum boys wanted to go. Khun Samran was to take them out to the practice site, Rajamangkala stadium, and he asked if I wanted to go along. Of course, I said yes, I very much wanted to go. It was in the cards for this to be a great experience.

A week prior to the trip, I was visiting the girls' home on Soi 40 and happened to mention the coming event. The house mom, Jai, also a football fan, was excited that our boys were to have the opportunity. As we were discussing the trip, one of the girls who had been on the camping trip, Pare, now fourteen years old, heard us talking and came up to me, frantically begging, "Uncle Tom, can I go? I want to go see them. I can play football."

I didn't know how to react. I thought it was a good idea. Pare was definitely physically active. She was one of the energy forces in the group dancing lessons that we had organized for the kids. I looked at Jai and saw she was a bit reserved about the idea. Jai told her it might be okay, but we would have to check with administration staff to see how the trip was being organized. As we talked afterward, Jai told me that she would check with the senior staff. I gave her the schedule for the bus to leave the Mercy Centre the following week. It would be just after lunch and the kids would have to get permission to take off school for that afternoon. I left thinking it would be arranged.

On the big day, when I went down from my desk at the Mercy Centre to join the boys on the bus, Pare, the Soi 40 girl, wasn't there. I asked Khun Samran, who was a graduate in sports education and definitely one who loved the beautiful game. He said he didn't know. He hadn't been told anything. It was time to go.

We went out to the practice session, and it was simply fabulous. The Thai teams never make it onto the world stage in international competitions. They only occasionally make it to the top of the Asian competitions. They were still doing the drills when we got to the field, and I saw why they had limited success outside of Asia. It was obvious watching that these were great athletes, running, jumping, twisting, turning, handling the ball beautifully all the way. However, only a few of them were bigger than me. At five feet ten inches tall, I left my American football dreams behind in high school. There may be great players of short stature in the competitive professional football world, the famed Messi, the legendary Maradona, but it is overall a game in which size counts as well as speed.

It didn't matter. The Mercy boys, standing on the sacred football grounds, were rapt with attention. The bonus event was that after the practice session, the coach brought his team over and introduced them to the boys. Oh, joy! The players talked to the boys, teasing them, asking how well they played, and then offered to show them some ball-handling tips. I remember in particular one boy about nine, who was watching it all but once in a while would look over at me with that kid's expression of wonder on his face. *Isn't this neat, Uncle Tom?* Yes, it was. The ball handling tips and drills were popular, but then we went on to the activity that would have the boys buzzing in the bus all the way home.

The star player at that time, Kiatisuk, nicknamed Zico, explained that one important step remained after they scored a goal. It was the celebration. Then Zico demonstrated his usual goal celebration. With a running start, he did a full-fledged aerial somersault, which he then continued with an arms-extended airplane run, weaving back and forth until he finished by sliding on his knees, holding his hands to the sky.

It was simply smashing. He demonstrated the steps again and did the leap and run, and the Mercy boys were shouting along. Don't just make a goal. Do it with flair. Important lesson. He was great.

The whole national team was great in their treatment of the boys. We had a short show of several of the boys attempting the somersault move, with little success and a few glorious failures. No embarrassment for them, but definitely a cause for laughs all around. It was a happy group of boys. I was really glad I had tagged along.

At the same time, I was upset that Pare wasn't there. A few days later, I went over to Soi 40 and asked Jai. She was also unhappy but told me the administrator, a senior woman staffer, was quite clear in not giving permission. "Girls don't play football."

I apologized to Pare, but she told me, "It's okay, Uncle Tom," using a very disappointed tone. I think one thing all slum kids, all poor kids around the world, learn how to say is "It's okay." They get used to the world letting them down.

The world has changed much since that event, and I'm happy to say that Mercy has moved on to include girls in the football picture. There is a school in Phuket, Thailand that combines a youth football program with the normal school curriculum. The school is the Youth Football Home Foundation Phuket. The school offers scholarships for the Mercy kids who display sports ability, to attend, receive training, and participate in competition while living on campus and attending school. Mercy readily accepted the offer. Today there are ten Mercy kids at the school, seven boys and three girls.

Chapter Twelve

THE HEROES

T he problem with making any sort of list is that necessarily, in the end, it's subjective. The list here is from my point of view and must therefore leave out those I didn't have extensive contact with. At the same time, it doesn't seem right to fail to acknowledge those heroes, children and adults, whom I had contact with and who impressed me so much during my time at Mercy.

Mercy Kids

The Mercy kids, those thousands that came to live at Mercy over the past fifty years, are the real heroes. In most societies, we say that the children who suffer misfortune are not to blame. In Thailand, possibly in any Buddhist country, some people say differently. In my first year at Mercy, my former secretary from the business world phoned me. She had mentioned to a friend that I had volunteered at Mercy. She said her friend was interested in seeing and gaining an understanding of what Mercy was. My secretary asked me if I would take her friend down to visit. I said yes immediately. To my mind, it seemed a great opportunity to attract a volunteer, a young Thai professional woman, who could work with the girls. I viewed the possibility as something comparable to the Big Sister program in the U.S.

On the chosen date, I picked the lady up and we drove over to Mercy. Even before we got to the Mercy Centre, she was getting an education akin to what I had experienced months before. I could sense her drawing back into her seat as we encountered the dismal gray concrete storage buildings, run-down shops, and working equipment of the port area. As we turned into the crowded, narrow road through the Jet Sip Rai slum, she was craning her head, looking around. There was trash scattered here and there on the closely packed street. She registered without word the battered appearance of the shop fronts, which were intersected by narrow sidewalk openings, giving glimpses of dingy wooden shack houses, with rusted sheet metal roofs, and open drainage ditches running along the narrow sidewalks. This was evidence of life lived at a lower level, well out of her sturdy middle-class experience.

When we arrived at Mercy, it was about the time the kids were coming home from school. After we parked, we went and just sat for a while on the bench in the entranceway. My thought was she could have the experience of the smiling, excited kids coming through, home from school. To me, the enthusiasm and high spirits of the kids were a joy. I loved it. She was quiet. Then I gave her a short tour, showing her the AIDS ward from a distance. I told her I understood that the AIDS program was not for her. The focus of the tour was the art room, the kid's sleeping rooms, and a look at the preschool up close. She had little reaction, but I wasn't surprised. It was a lot to take in on a first visit.

As we were leaving and I was driving her back to the pickup point, she finally had something to say. First, she thanked me for taking her to see Mercy. Then she said, "I always wondered what *they* were like."

I was stunned. The word *they* in the comment was emphasized. The connotation was clear. It meant *those others* in a negative sense. It was a very simple remark, but in the Buddhist context, it carried so much meaning. Life is about karma. The *they* designated in her comment were the poor and their children. She was voicing the somewhat commonly held belief that the children, and the residents of the slum, were guilty of offenses in the past life and responsible for their suffering in the current life. I have been impressed, over the years, with many of the tenets of Buddhism, and the depth of belief I encountered in Thailand, but my thinking is that the children are innocent. My understanding of Buddhist belief is that all the world is a family, but it seems, for some people, not all family members are equal. She said no more about the visit. It was clear to me that she wouldn't volunteer. No big sister for the girls. She wouldn't be back.

The kids fight to overcome that prejudice. The Mercy kids are the primary group I think of as heroes. As Fr. Joe says, they come out of the slum "kicking open the door" to a better life. I'm sure that's true around the world. Give a poor kid some attention, some love, and a supportive environment, and they will respond. They will grow and overcome the mistreatment they had lived through before they found a refuge. Instead of trying to sleep in a schoolroom overnight to avoid abuse at home or running to the streets to beg and hide from sight, when offered a protective, nourishing shelter, they will respond.

The Mercy kids, most of them abused in one way or another, have always taken a hand up when given it. Mercy kids have gone on to college, both in Thailand and overseas. One girl gained a science doctorate in the U.S. Another girl became a black belt tae kwon do instructor and a bit of a rock star to her many Mercy friends. More importantly overall, Mercy kids stayed safe and finished high school, in itself a notable achievement for the poorest of the poor.

When I think of the years immediately preceding my going to Mercy and knocking on Fr. Joe's door to volunteer, it seems to me that I was moving in a direction I couldn't really understand at the time. *Driven is a* phrase Fr. Joe uses describing his own pathway from "terribly poor" beginnings into the priesthood, to Thailand and Laos, to Bangkok, then to the slaughterhouse parish and, with Sr. Maria, the founding of Mercy. To me. it wasn't an accidental journey . I believe he was moving along in a direction prompted by his subconscious being, as we all may do, if we can just be quiet for a moment.

Fr. Joe wanted to serve the poor and their children, and he has done so in a noteworthy fashion. But he is not alone. Sr. Maria, Khun Usanee, and the Mercy staff, all sharing the same goal, banded together to make Mercy the special refuge of love that it is. They don't have jobs, rather they have deeply held vocations to aid the poor and their children. After I met Fr. Joe and worked with him and the staff of Mercy over the years, I came to understand that being drawn to Mercy was, for me, the path to overcoming the PTSD, anger, and bitterness I carried with me for virtually all my life. Simply put, somehow entering a world of children suffering from the worst forms of PTSD and trying to help to them, worked to redeem the PTSD I had carried and wrestled with for so long. You can never forget, but you can come to terms with yourself. That is the gift the children give. In trying to ease their pain, you can work through yours.

There are many other Mercy homes in the world. There are other sites in other cities to which children in need can run. One can ask, what are the elements of its structure that make you feel that the Mercy home in Bangkok is special? To me, it starts with the Mercy schools and teachers. These are the teachers who are the first line of care for many of the kids. Mercy would not be the refuge that it is if it didn't have the base of the preschools to build on. The kids come to the schools and the teachers are slum moms who understand them and love them. These are women who are poor themselves, and many also come from the poorest of backgrounds.

Mercy is very much a woman's organization. I would guess the number of men at present comprise about ten to fifteen per cent of the staff. Many of the Mercy staff and counselors are heroes, but it seems to me that it is the women, the nourishing feminine side, who bring the family love to the house. I would put these teachers, along with the children who responded to their care, at the head of the list of those I came away feeling were heroes.

What I will try to do next is impossible. I will fail and leave many heroes out. But I feel obligated to try. To be of use to any social welfare organization, especially in a foreign country, a volunteer must depend on the openness and support of the professional staff and other, more experienced, volunteers to help them find a productive role. These are the people I was lucky enough to have help from during my time at Mercy. The staff are the people who I witnessed providing care in my fourteen years there. I want to note them publicly. They are of differing backgrounds, virtually all of them coming from an impoverished setting themselves, but they were all drawn to Mercy for the noblest of reasons, the love of children.

As a combat soldier, I served in Vietnam with men who were termed heroes. Some sacrificed their lives to save brothers in arms. I identify with that courage. However, during my time at Mercy, I was to learn of another kind of heroism. That is the courage to work in the most difficult circumstances, with little material reward, yet to come back day after day and share the best you have with children in need. The children's smiles are the reward these women receive.

Mercy Staff

Khun Usanee is the staff member with whom I had the most involvement at Mercy, and, after that, with the Little Birds Foundation. We first met when I wandered into the Mercy AIDS hospice during my third month at Mercy, searching for a way to be helpful. She is, as are most of the staff, a strong Buddhist. She was the patient lady who introduced me to the Thai medical student who had been visiting from the U.S. Usanee came to Mercy a few years out of nursing school in the U.K. in 1992 and was responsible for developing the HIV/AIDS hospice and program. That program was the first private HIV/AIDS hospice in Thailand. Under her direction, Mercy then originated a home-based care program to assist families to care for AIDS patients at home. Mercy's HIV/AIDS program evolved until it was eventually recognized by the Thai government, fifteen years later, as the premier program of its type in Thailand. We worked together extensively during her leadership of the post-tsunami reconstruction program. Usanee served as Mercy's executive director as we worked to regain our balance from the financial and operational disruption caused by the tsunami relief program.

Finally, Khun Usanee motivated the establishment of the Little Birds group which led to the independent Little Birds Foundation of today. Little Birds was started to provide guidance and support for living with HIV/AIDS to the young adults who were leaving Mercy to enter the community. Today, Little Birds is recognized and accepted by the Thai government and has won awards as the leading group for HIV/AIDS kids and young adults in Thailand. The beginnings of the group, over ten years ago, owed to Khun Usanee's vision and compassion for these kids. While we worked on the tsunami reconstruction projects, Robert Hermelin, a key staffer for Hong Kong & Shanghai Bank (HKSB) and a donor for several projects, came to me and asked if he and HKSB could nominate Usanee for the CNN heroes' program. I thought she deserved the recognition and asked her about it. Her answer was a clear no. She, like Sr. Maria, is not in search of public recognition. Without her permission, I recognize her contributions to the children of Mercy here.

Jai was the house mom at Soi 40 when I first came to Mercy. Soi 40 was a house of love and joy for the girls. Jai would oversee the girls' development into young ladies. She knew them and loved them deeply. It was only with her assistance that I could get started at trying to be useful to Mercy. She explained Mercy to me. She allowed me to be a helper with projects, camping, dancing, and others that the girls wanted as a relief from their daily life. Jai and I continue to be friends. She now works with the Fr. Ray Brennan Orphanage in Pattaya, Thailand.

Khun Samran serves as the leader in the Street Children's Outreach program. His devotion to his work and the kids he helps is outstanding. He accepted and encouraged my efforts to help kids I found on the streets. As the staffer who regularly visits the juvenile detention facility, he has had to weather some discouraging responses from its administrators. However, he is a strong Buddhist and he keeps calm in those difficult conditions. He has brought home to Mercy many boys that Mercy was able to assist and give a better chance at life.

Krue Nang (Narisaraporn) I remember as the nightrider motorcycle woman. She would ride out at 10 p.m. to Sanam Luang, an area where street kids gathered, so she could advise them on caring for themselves and offer them shelter if they were ready for it. She speaks little English, and our work times did not overlap, so I know her just from seeing her occasionally in the office and then listening to Khun Usanee's strong praise. Krue Nang came to Mercy from Buri Ram, a farm village in the northeast of Thailand, with just her backpack and a desire to help children in need. She is called Mae (mother) by the kids and protects those living on the street or under bridges. She finds them day jobs, enters them in school, and ensures they get second chances. In 2013, she was chosen as Bangkok's Best Street Worker in Action by the Thai government.

Kuhn Prong was a key worker in the tsunami reconstruction effort. She was a leading contact and compassionate with the many women who had suffered the loss of their home and oft-times of a child. Prong was the pioneer in going to the Mo Ken village on Koh Lao in 2006, and she leads the care and integration into Thai society for those in the village to this day. She stays at the Mercy Home in the port city of Ranong, the mainland fishing port closest to the island, and oversees the kids during this time of Covid. There are sixty-five Mo Ken children going to school on the island. In the Mercy Home in Ranong, there are fifteen of the older Mo Ken children who attend public junior high and high school in Ranong. They would normally go back to see their families on Koh Lao each weekend, but due to Covid precautions, they are presently unable to do so. She is also known to the Mo Ken kids as Mae or mother Prong.

Other Mercy social workers have received community service awards from the Thai Ministry of Social Development and Welfare. I found them outstanding in their devotion to the kids and their duties at Mercy. One is Khun Kittisuk, who went from being a "train station" street kid in Bangkok to Mercy. He grew to be a drug addiction counselor at Mercy and then to serve as the house dad at the Mercy boy's farm home at the edge of Bangkok.

Another is Khun Watecharapol (Mos), a key hospice and social worker at mercy. He also came from the streets, guided to Mercy by a Catholic brother. At Mercy, he is known for his gentle nature as he tends to the AIDS patients and visits them in their homes. It was Khun Mos who patiently guided me during my early, uneducated efforts at the Mercy Hospice.

Then there are Khun Chutima, Khun Tan, and Khun Mo, nurses in the Mercy Hospice during my early days there. For over ten years, and through endless counseling sessions, they have worked with the Little Birds, advising and boosting them along the path to a sustainable adult life.

Volunteers

Over the years, Mercy has attracted many hundreds of volunteers. Most are well-meaning. They come to Mercy to give of themselves and, when they do so, they find that Mercy gives back. How do I separate out a few of these?

There is one very simple standard. I felt these were people whose spirit was truly moved and who were captivated by the kids. Also, these volunteers weren't visitors who came for a few weeks or a month, but those who dedicated a significant part of their life to Mercy. Below are some volunteers who I came to know well, who demonstrated their love for the kids, and who impressed me with their spirit of caring at Mercy. My apologies to those whose work I have failed to acknowledge due to my limitations.

Tew Bunnag is an author, a teacher, and in most recent years, one who provides counseling and emotional care to the dying. Tew grew up in Bangkok but lives in Spain today. I would see him at Mercy on the many occasions when he came back to Bangkok to see to the care of his mother as she grew older. Tew is highly respected by many of the senior staff of Mercy as a mentor. I associate his times at Mercy, and there were many of them over the years including the tsunami reconstruction time, most often with the AIDS hospice and the HIV/AIDS children. He spoke to them and counseled them in their illness and, at times, in their dying. To endure that pain, to ensure a dying child's comfort, is the ultimate in love.

John Padorr's time at Mercy dates back to the time I arrived. However, we didn't come to know each other well until I came to work in the office on assuming the financial reporting duties during the tsunami reconstruction period. John, having been in the advertising field over the years, has been responsible for Mercy's public communications. That includes the outstanding website at www.mercycentre.org. He is an excellent writer. If it was written at Mercy, it was probably written by John, except of course for Fr. Joe's monthly newsletters. More importantly, as with all the volunteers who I came to respect, John cared for the kids. He would often sit on the bench by the entrance to Mercy as the kids came home from school. He would chat with many of them and amazed me in that he came to know the names of many more of the kids than any of us, possibly including Fr. Joe. The most wounded of the kids found a special place in his heart.

Mary McLean, a Canadian, was a volunteer for a period covering two years in 2005 and 2006, between college and graduate school. A short period compared to some other volunteers, but she loved the kids and made a difference. She roomed in the girl's house at Soi 40, ate her meals there, and was on hand at all hours when the girls needed an older sister to talk to. As a musician, she provided a boost to the Mercy music program. After Joop Chang died, I wanted to do something special with the dolphin necklace I had given Joop that the staff had returned to me. I gave it to Mary. who had cared for Joop so much.

Mike and Deborah Simms are a retired couple from California who volunteered for two months at a time each year from 2003 to 2010. They brought unique skills. More importantly, their answer to "Could you . . . ?" when Mercy required something was always *yes*. Mike is a former fire captain, with a home construction background and strong woodworking skills. He started a woodworking shop at Mercy and acted as a teacher and role model for the Mercy boys. He cooked a Thanksgiving dinner for the staff on one occasion and, on another, organized a group of the boys to visit the local fire station and learn the basics of a firefighter's life. Deborah helped to refine the written materials at Mercy and as an assistant in the kindergarten program and English language instructor for both the kids and staff. They both assisted Sr. Joan Evans with her weekly milk runs to aid new mothers in the slums.

John MacTaggart is a medical equipment sales executive who has resided in Bangkok for over twenty years. John, early on, took an interest in the HIV/AIDS hospice and program at Mercy. He came to know all the staff and the kids. When appropriate, then and today, he provides a medical sounding board for the Mercy AIDS staff when they are considering issues that confront the kids. He has journeyed home to his roots in Scotland and raised money for Mercy programs. John loves the kids, and I have joined him in tears at more than one Mercy kid's cremation at the slum temple, Wat Saphan.

Fr. Joe and Khun Prong at flooded Mercy school. Credit Mercy Centre

Mercy boys as Monks, Khun Samran on left and
Khun Teng on third from right. Credit Mercy Centre

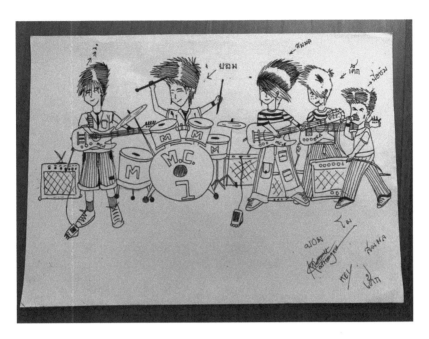

Drawing of the Baby Ghosts band. Credit to Gee and Mary McLean

Early Days, Mercy Preschool. Credit Mercy Centre

Mercy Preschool Graduation. Credit Yoon Ki Kim

Ekamai Construction Camp School. Credit Mercy Centre

Slum housing on Canal. Credit Mercy Centre

Rail line community Jet Sip Rai. Credit Yoon Ki Kim

After Slum Fire, Rom Klao. Credit Mercy Centre

Fr. Joe and Sr. Maria. Credit Mercy Centre

Kru Nang and Street Kids Under the Bridge. Credit Mercy Centre

Ink, 13 year old girl Muay Thai champion, preparing for match.
Credit Yoon Ki Kim

Ink, resting after training. Credit Yoon Ki Kim

ACKNOWLEDGMENTS

Many, many, thanks to my good friends, Jack Tieder, who has passed away in recent years, and former Deputy Assistant Secretary of State Matt Daley. They stepped in to give much-needed direction to the U.S. foundation, Mercy Centre USA, at a time of need and Matt continues to work in supporting the Little Bird's program. Also, thanks to the proud Naval Academy graduate Bob Bishop for his valuable assistance and hard work editing my initial text, and Khun Prawina and Khun Nitaya in the Mercy office who helped me to gather background and check my facts. Finally, I must pay homage to Yoon Ki Kim, an outstanding photographer whose love for the kids has led him to document several generations of family life in the Klong Toey slums. His black and white pictures bring the slum families to life. He taught me much about life in the slums.

There is a phrase that is somewhat overused now, but I think still appropriate on certain occasions, "It takes a village." Fr. Joe, Sister Maria, kids, teachers, staff, and volunteers have worked together as a village, as a community for children, to make Mercy a true refuge of love.

MERCY AWARDS AND RECOGNITION

Over the past forty years, Mercy has received many awards. I've included a partial list of these below.

2012—The National Human Rights Commission (NHRC) of Thailand gave Fr. Joe its annual award recognizing those national heroes who have the courage to stand up and fight for the rights of those who cannot fight for themselves.

2009—Fr. Joe was named as the Child Protection Ambassador to Thailand for 2009 in an award presented by Prime Minister Abhisit Vejjajiva. Fr. Joe was the first foreign resident of Thailand ever to receive this honorary title.

2004—Mercy received the award for Outstanding Citizenship for social work and community development in the field of HIV/AIDS. The award was decided by the Thai Red Cross AIDS Research Centre.

2004—Fr. Joe received the Lifetime Achievement award from the Thai government for Mercy's programs in the field of protection of mothers and children.

1998—Mercy received the Special Achievement award from the National Council of Thailand for Child Development.

1997—Mercy received the United Nation's ESCAP HRD award as the best NGO among forty-one Asian nations based on the quality and sustainability of Mercy programs and their positive impact on the community.

Please consider a donation to the Little Birds Foundation: The details are as follows:

Bank Account:

Bank Name: Siam Commercial Bank (SCB)
Gateway Ekamai Branch (OC:5331)
982/22 Sukhumvit Road
Phrakhanong Sub District
Khlong Toei District
Bangkok
10110
Account Name: Foundation Little Birds Youth Network
Account Number: 4210307717
Swift Code: SICOTHBK

BANGKOK BLOG

Some years back I would write and post the occasional blog entry online. I abandoned that practice as I got busy with my website and my writing for publication. From those previous postings, here is an article on life in the Bangkok slums I thought might be of interest in conjunction with Mercy's heroes. There is more on the website: www.tomcrowleybooks.com

Warriors of the Bangkok Slums

There exists, in the crowded squalor of slum huts, open sewage drains, under expressway overheads, alongside dirty train tracks, in the poorest areas of this sprawling city of eleven million people, a tribe of warriors whose training for combat starts early in life and never ends. It's a family-oriented clan that passes the warrior tradition down from generation to generation. In all cases, these families have no wealth other than this golden tradition. The members of this group have homes, albeit, for the most part, these are squatter's slum shacks thrown up on land alongside the railroad tracks. Though their family lives are important, they work at a variety of basic labor and security jobs and the children go to school every day, it is the training ground that is very much the center of their existence and identity. The training ground is a bit of open-air space alongside the railroad tracks and underneath the expressway. It's a small lot, no more than twenty meters wide and thirty meters long. It's surrounded by a chain-link fence and has some rough concrete toilets built in a corner at one end. At the other end, taking up almost the full width, is the boxing ring, standard size, three feet above ground with a fence of ropes around the sides. Yes, the war that these warriors train for is the one to be fought with the ancient Thai combat art of Muay Thai.

There are fifteen children working out today on the eleven large, dilapidated kick bags hanging from four iron frames set up around the inside of the gym ground. The ground itself has a rubber covering over the concrete. What they have done, to emulate the composite floor covering of modern gyms, is cut up old truck tires, available from a cross-country truck lot nearby, flatten them out as much as possible and make that the floor for the gym to protect the children, to some extent, when they take falls. The tires are not flattened very well, and it is easy to trip on edges and bumps sticking up when just walking around the gym.

I have been introduced to this camp, in a slum area named Penang 96, by the Korean photographer, Yoon Ki Kim. Mr. Kim has been following and photographing the lives of this warrior clan for fifteen years and is planning a book chronicling the lives of three generations of one of the families. Mr. Kim's classic black and white photos are an important part of my nonfiction book, *Bangkok Pool Blues,* about the night people inhabiting the emerging pool culture that has grown up in Bangkok over the past ten years. The camp is open every day, except Sunday, from 4 p.m. to 7 p.m. The children come after school and train until the camp closes.

There are about six older males, most in their fifties, in attendance, former fighters, all now carrying excess weight and no longer in the boxing form they once were. One older guy who looks to be in his sixties, but wearing Muay Thai trunks and gear, is sparring and playing around with the kids. He has a punched-out look and manner, both gruff and kindly, that reminds me of the trainer for Rocky Balboa in the famed *Rocky* motion picture series. It's after 5 p.m. when we arrive and the kids are sweating heavily, having worked for over an hour already, in the dense Bangkok heat and the dead, almost noxious air underneath the expressway. However, what strikes you almost immediately, after getting through the initial introductions to Kru (teacher) Preaw and the older males in attendance, is both the intensity of the kids in training and the happiness they show at being here, in the holiest of holies, Kru Preaw's Muay Thai training camp at Penang ninety-six.

In discussion with Kru Preaw, the family angle becomes evident. He is in his late fifties; over thirty years ago, he was a competition fighter taking on the best at the famed Lumpinee Muay Thai stadium, the pinnacle of Muay Thai competition in Thailand. After that, he trained his son Be and others, mostly relatives, some starting to learn as young as the age of ten. Now Be is in his thirties, working as a security guard. Now Kru Preaw is training, along with many others, his grandchildren. His granddaughter Ink, who is fourteen has won a national championship in a children's Muay Thai competition, and his grandson Chuan, who is thirteen, shows competitive promise. There are certainly more offspring and more championships in the offing for this family.

All in all, it adds up for me to a very impressive story, combining poverty and the poorest of children. They are possessed of a strong can-do attitude, which erupts periodically in smiles and laughter, while at the same time, they are working with incredible diligence at learning one of the hardest of martial arts. These kids may be poor, but they are rich in family and in the self-confidence their training brings. It's enough to make you feel sorry for the rich kids who may never be so fully challenged and thus allowed to experience the inner strength they are capable of.

OTHER WORKS ON MERCY

Books:

Title: *The Open Gates of Mercy*
Author: Fr. Joe Maier
ISBN: 6167503141
Publisher: Heaven Lake Press, Pub Date: August 1, 2012

Title: *The Gospel of Father Joe*
Author: Greg Barrett
ISBN: 978-0-470-25863-7
Publisher: Josey-Bass, Pub Date: 2008

Title: *Welcome to the Bangkok Slaughterhouse*
Author: Fr. Joe Maier
ISBN: 962-8734-76-8
Publisher: Periplus Editions (HK) Ltd., Asia Books Co. (Thailand) Ltd.
Pub Date: 2005

Videos:

Title: Mercy in the Slums of Bangkok

Type of Source: Video by Bill Whelan, the composer of River Dance, 2014.

URL: https://www.youtube.com/watch?v=Jn6YnbXTG1Y&t=1s

This highlights the plight of the street children. The narration by Mercy staff and volunteers is excellent and to the point.

Title: The Slum Priest—Fr. Joe

Type of Source: Peabody-Award-winning video by PBS Religion and Ethics, narrated by Phil Jones, 2004.

URL: https://www.youtube.com/watch?v=ojK-lssbOok&t=21s

The news photography is powerful. Phil Jones does a masterful job of interviewing Fr. Joe and some of the Mercy staff.

Title: Father Joe and the Bangkok Slaughterhouse Documentary

Type of Source: Video by James Lingwood, Australia, 2008.

URL: https://www.youtube.com/watch?v=1e4kaTG5Vjk

Professional and evocative, this highlights Mercy's HIV/AIDS program.